The Low-Fat Kitchen

Acknowledgements

All of my recipes for this cookbook were created in the the test kitchen at the Los Angeles Times for my Low-Fat Cooking column which has been running in the food section for the last five years. I would like to thanks the members of the Los Angeles Times Test Kitchen, Mayi Brady and Maria Galaviz, for their support and enthusiasm. All photographs were taken in the photo studio at the Los Angeles Times by Times staff photographers. A special thanks to the staff photographers for their creativity and cooperation in our weekly photo shoots. I would also like to thank food editor Laurie Ochoa for her direction and excellent editing of the book and Carla Lazzareschi for making the project happen. A special thanks to Tamas for his complete honesty and patience in tasting and evaluating my recipes over the years.

THE LOW-FAT KITCHEN

RECIPES AND TIPS FOR HEALTHFUL, GREAT-TASTING MEALS

By Donna Deane
Los Angeles Times
Test Kitchen Director

Los Angeles Times

Los Angeles Times

Book Development Manager: Carla Lazzareschi
Food Section Editor: Laurie Ochoa
Copy Editor: Kathy Gosnell
Nutritional Analysis: Bruce Henstell
Design: Tom Trapnell

ISBN 1-883792-22-3
Copyright © Los Angeles Times 1998
Published by the Los Angeles Times
Times Mirror Square
All rights reserved. No part of this book may be reproduced
without the written permission of the publisher.

First printing May 1998

Printed in the U.S.A.

Contents

Introduction 7
Secrets of the Low-Fat Kitchen 8
Reading Nutrition Labels 9
Low-Fat Baking Techniques 10
Low-Fat Kitchen Essentials 11
Low-Fat Cooking Techniques 15

Breakfast and Brunch
Potato Frittata 17
Polenta Pancakes 18
Apple Pancakes 19
Almond Brown Rice Breakfast Drink 20
Berry Blast 20

Appetizers
Oven Fried Zucchini 21
Basil and Prosciutto Wrapped Shrimp ... 22
Spanakopita 23
Caviar-Stuffed Potatoes 24
Baked Eggrolls 25
Couscous-Stuffed Grape Leaves 26
Artichoke Pesto 27
Ahi Tuna Bites 28

Soups
Turkey Soup 29
Chinese Dumpling Soup 30
California Chile Soup 31
Curried Sweet Potato Soup 32
Escarole Chicken Soup 33
Chinese Vegetable Soup 34
Salmon Chowder 35

Salads
Nonfat Thousand Island Dressing 36
Nonfat Ranch-Style Dressing 37
Nonfat Green Goddess Dressing 37
Orzo Chopped Salad 38
Dilled Potato and Haricots Verts Salad .. 39
Roasted Eggplant Salad 40
Baja Squid Salad 41
Shrimp and Garlic Coleslaw 41
Potato Salad with Cilantro Vinaigrette ... 42
Fresh Vegetable Toss 43
Shrimp and Artichoke Quinoa Salad 44
Black-Eyed Peas and Mustard Greens ... 45
Fresh Garden Vegetable Salad 46
Roasted Beet Salad 47
Brown Rice and Vegetable Salad 48
Oven-Fried Chicken Salad 49
Farmers Market Salad 50
Shredded Chicken Salad 51
Winter Fruit Salad 52

Pizza, Pasta, Pane
Pizza Pomodoro 53
Spaghetti with Charred Tomato Sauce ... 54
Stuffed Cannelloni 55
Swiss Chard and Tofu over Capellini 56
Fresh Tomato Lasagna 57
Rigatoni with Portabellos and Peppers .. 58
Pad Thai Noodles 59
Olive-Yogurt Turban 60
Skinny Bread Sticks 61
Double Corn Muffins 62
California Wrap 63
Summer "Egg" Salad Sandwich 64

Meat, Fish and Poultry
Mixed Vegetable and Beef Stir-Fry 65
Grilled Flank Stead Adobo 66
Shrimp Fried Rice 67
Steamed Salmon with Tarragon Sauce ... 68
Chinese Rock Cod with Vegetables 69
Paillard of Swordfish 70
Shrimp Tostada 71
Twice-Baked Potatoes Brandade 72
Scallops in Cream Sauce 73

Lavash Rolled with Smoked Tuna 74
Low-Fat '50s Tuna Noodle Casserole 75
Red Snapper Marinated in Sake Lees 76
Seafood in Black Bean Sauce 77
Chilled Florentine Turkey Terrine 78
Dilled Turkey Meat Balls 79
Turkey Fajitas 80
Turkey and Vegetable Rice Bowl 81
Low-Fat Turkey Chili 82
Turkey Meat Balls in Red Sauce 83
Asian Minced Turkey with Tofu 84
Chicken Enchiladas 85

VEGETABLES AND OTHER SIDE DISHES

Brussel Sprouts in Garlic Cream Sauce .. 86
Hungarian-Style Yellow Beans 87
Balsamic Roasted Squash 88
Savory Baked Sweet Potatoes 89
Herb Roasted Potatoes and Peppers 91
Cabbage and Potatoes 90
Eggplant Stack 91
Stuffed Chayote Squash 92
Vegetable Hungarian Lecso 93
Vegetable Curry 94
Pilaf with Assorted Vegetables 95
Stuffed Tomatoes 96
Sweet-and-Sour Tofu 97

DESSERTS

Cranberry Ice 98
Honeydew Ice 99
Mexican Chocolate Ice 100
Date Bites 101
Chewy Oatmeal-Cherry Cookies 102
Lemon Bars 102
Anise Meringue Kisses 103
Pine Nut Crisps 103
Rosemary Biscotti 104
Chocolate Pudding with Bananas 105
Bavarian Cream 105
Caffe Latte Custard 106
Creamy Rice Pudding 107
Lemon Brulée 108
Fresh Berry Cobbler 109
Baked Apple-Oat Crunch 110
Ginger Pumpkin Pie 110
Peaches and "Cream" Pie 111
June Blueberry Pie 112
Lemon Dream Cake 113
Chocolate Carrot Cake 115
Very Berry Cake 116
Pink Peppercorn Angel Food Cake 117
Chocolate Cloud Cake 118
Avocado Cake with Dates 119

Index 121

Introduction

IF QUICK WEIGHT LOSS IS YOUR primary objective, you might as well put this book down now. This is not a diet book but a collection of great-tasting recipes that will help you lead a healthful, low-fat lifestyle. Flavor is my first concern in developing recipes for the weekly column I write for the Los Angeles Times Food section and for this book. If it doesn't taste good, I don't want to eat it.

Deprivation diets may get the pounds off fast, but they won't help you keep the weight off. Over and over, research shows that the most effective way to maintain a sensible body weight is simply to maintain a sensible diet. Common sense is more important than kitchen scales and charts.

If you keep a Low-Fat Kitchen—stocked with wonderful fresh foods, with a few useful gadgets and a little technical know-how on your part—you won't have to think too much about your diet. Eating and cooking good food will come naturally.

The problem for most people is that they are stuck in high-fat eating and cooking habits. A tablespoon of butter automatically goes in the skillet whenever anything is sautéed; oil is always used to dress salads; a large piece of meat is considered a necessary centerpiece of a meal. In this book, I hope to help you explore a few alternatives. A well-seasoned cast-iron skillet, for instance, needs very little and sometimes no added fat for cooking. Lemon and other fruit juices brightened with fresh herbs make wonderful dressings. And meat *can* take a supporting role at dinner.

When your daily meals are based on seasonal produce, fresh fish and good cuts of meat flavored with fresh herbs, spices and chiles, the food that comes out of your own Low-Fat Kitchen will always make you happy.

—*Donna Deane*

Secrets of the Low-Fat Kitchen

Use less of the best. Select high-quality ingredients—especially extra-virgin olive oil, high-grade vanilla extract, fruits and vegetables in season and good cheeses—for maximum flavor.

• Use meat as a condiment rather than as the main ingredient. Add vegetables and grains for substance.

• Choose lean cuts of beef. Look for the word "loin" or "round" on the package; these are often the leanest. Eye of round or top round comes in at 4 grams of fat per 3-ounce cooked portion followed by top sirloin, round tip, roasted, and full cut round, broiled, at 6 grams of fat per 3-ounce cooked portion. Tenderloin, porterhouse, T-bone, rib and flank steak all contain 9 grams of fat. A 3-ounce cooked portion of veal is laced with 5.6 ounces of fat.

• Don't automatically eliminate pork. The leanest cut of pork is the tenderloin, which has a low 4.1 grams of fat per 3-ounce cooked portion. Boneless sirloin chops are reasonable at 5.7 grams of fat per 3-ounce cooked portion and boneless loin roast has 6.4 grams of fat per 3-ounce cooked portion. A pork rib roast comes in at 8.6 grams per 3-ounce cooked portion.

• Trim fat from lamb before cooking. Loin chops that have been well trimmed have about 8 ounces of fat per 3-ounce cooked portion, and roasted leg of lamb has about 7 grams of fat.

• Look for white-meat poultry. Look for skinless, boneless chicken breasts, turkey tenderloins and turkey breast. Remove poultry skin after cooking instead of before to get the juiciest flavor; you'll cut about 5.5 grams of fat per 3-ounce cooked portion. A skinless chicken drumstick has 4 grams fat, compared to 9 grams with the skin on.

• When using ground turkey or chicken, check to be sure it is white meat, not dark. If you're not sure, ask your butcher to grind it fresh for you.

• Choose fish that is less oily. Sea bass, red snapper, sole, flounder and cod are good choices.

• Trim meats of fat before cooking. If meat is well-trimmed, 50 percent of the fat in the portion you're using can be eliminated.

• Fresh fruit and vegetable salsas make great accompaniments to main dish items and can be made fat-free.

• Increase herbs and seasonings in a low-fat dish to compensate for the flavor lost from the reduced fat.

• The addition of fresh minced or crushed

What's in a Label?

The Nutrition Facts label on most food packages gives a breakdown of nutrients and the per-serving percent of what the government calls Daily Values. These are based on a 2,000- to 2,500-calorie diet for adults and children over two years of age.

Serving sizes have been standardized for similar foods in recent years so you can compare labels.

The label provides a listing of nutrients in the product given in grams. A parallel column gives the percentage each nutrient will fill in your daily quota. For instance, if a label reads 3 grams of fat at 5% Daily Value, it means one serving will give you 5% of the fat you need in your diet for that day. No more than 30 percent of the calories you consume in a day should come from fat.

Here are a few of the standardized definitions of the terms manufacturers are allowed to use on their products:

Fat-Free: less than 1/2 gram fat per serving. Used interchangeably with the terms "100 percent fat-free" and "non-fat."

100% Fat-Free: meets requirements for Fat-Free (less than 1/2 gram fat per serving).

Low-Fat: 3 grams fat or less per serving.

Reduced-Fat: at least 25% less fat when compared with similar foods.

—% Fat-Free: meets requirements for Low-Fat. The percentage is based on the amount of fat (by weight) in 100 grams of food. Example: If 50 grams of food contain 2 1/2 grams fat, the food can be labeled "95% fat-free."

Saturated Fat-Free: less than 1/2 gram saturated fat per serving.

Low Saturated Fat: 1 gram or less saturated fat per serving and no more than 15 percent of calories from saturated fat.

Reduced Saturated Fat: at least 25 percent less saturated fat per serving when compared to a similar food.

Lean: packed seafood, game meat, cooked meat or cooked poultry with less than 10 grams total fat, less than 4 grams saturated fat and less than 95 milligrams cholesterol.

Extra Lean: contains less than 5 grams total fat, less than 2 grams saturated fat and less than 95 milligrams cholesterol per serving in 100 grams of food.

Source: American Dietetic Association

• • •

garlic is a great flavor booster.

• A light dusting of freshly grated Parmesan cheese, a squeeze of fresh lemon or lime juice, a touch of vinegar and a sprinkling of chopped fresh herbs are all good flavor enhancements for low-fat cooking.

• Toasting nuts intensifies their flavor, so you will need less.

• Toasting spices brings out their flavor. Toast whole spices, then grind them fresh for maximum flavor. A light heating of dried herbs in a skillet brings out the flavor.

• Dry spice rubs or spice blends add flavor without fat when smoothed onto the surface of meat and allowed to stand before cooking.

• Fruit- and herb-flavored vinegars can be used in marinades for meat, fish and poultry. Reduce fat (oil) in marinades to 1 tablespoon or less.

• When making oil-based salad dressings, replace about half the oil with reduced-fat chicken broth or fruit juices.

• When making creamy salad dressing, stir a little reduced-fat chicken broth into low-fat mayonnaise or mayonnaise blended

BAKING IN THE LOW-FAT KITCHEN

In baking, fruit purées can replace some or part of the fat traditionally called for in many recipes. To make your own purée, blend together 1 cup dried fruit with 6 tablespoons water and 1 teaspoon vanilla extract in a blender or food processor to make 3/4 cup purée. Fruit purées can also be purchased in supermarkets.
- Try using cake flour when baking low-fat products for a lighter texture.
- When baking, use chopped dried fruits instead of high-fat nuts or chocolate chips.
- Use cocoa instead of high-fat chocolate when baking. Cocoa also can be sprinkled over cakes or tortes for a lower-fat finishing touch.

• • •

with nonfat yogurt or nonfat sour cream.
- Use a slurry of cornstarch and water as a thickener rather then a buttery roux.
- Another roux alternative is to toast flour in a skillet until lightly browned for added flavor, then blend it with water until smooth. This technique adds a nutty flavor to sauces.
- Dust cakes with powdered sugar rather then rich frostings.
- Roasting vegetables at high heat caramelizes the sugar and adds sweetness along with flavor. You won't need extra butter or oil at the table to make the vegetables taste good.
- When preparing soups or stews, make them ahead of time, then chill them in the refrigerator so the fat can rise to the top. Just before reheating, remove the layer of fat that may be on the surface.
- Chill homemade stocks so that the maximum amount of fat can be removed. Also, chill canned broths so that any lingering fat can be removed.
- Stretch main dishes by serving them over unbuttered rice and noodles.
- Drained yogurt can take the place of cream cheese in some recipes.
- Use reduced-fat mayonnaise, nonfat sour cream and nonfat yogurt in salads or sandwich fillings.
- Use low-fat or nonfat products whenever possible.
- Canned white beans can be used to thicken some dressings and sauces. When puréed, they add a neutral thickening base with little fat.
- When using canned goods, always check the labels, even if you're buying a product you use often. The fat content varies from brand to brand and sometimes even from can to can in products from the same company.
- Use low-fat breads like bagels, English muffins, lavash, pita breads, French breads and corn tortillas in recipes and for accompaniments.
- Highly flavored condiments such as hoisin, soy sauce, oyster sauce, hot sauces and chile sauces add flavor with little added fat.
- It makes a difference when you take a few extra minutes to arrange your food on a plate or add a special garnish. It seems to make the meal more satisfying.

Essentials of a Low-Fat Kitchen Pantry

Brown rice syrup: Very similar to honey in consistency but doesn't have the overpowering flavor and isn't as sweet as honey. It is gluten-free and available in health food stores.

Cheese: Look for ones made with skim milk. When using nonfat cheese, be careful not to overheat it; because of its lack of fat, it can become tough. A few good cheese choices include:

Farmers cheese and feta cheese: Tangy in flavor, both are ideal low-fat cheeses to crumble over cooked dishes.

Low-fat ricotta: Regular ricotta has 24 grams of fat per cup, but low-fat and fat-free versions are available.

Mexican cotija: This is a lower-fat cheese that goes well with Mexican food and can be used in any dish in which a crumbly white cheese is needed.

Parmesan or Romano: A little grated Parmesan can go a long way. Buy a wedge and keep it on hand to grate over pastas and salads.

Skim milk mozzarella: This is about 2 grams lower in fat per 1 1/2-ounce serving than regular mozzarella.

Chicken and beef broths: Homemade stocks are always preferable if you have the time to make them. You can control the amount of salt, for one thing. Strain stocks after you make them and chill them overnight so the fat can rise to the top and you can easily skim it off. When using canned broths, choose low-sodium, reduced-fat broths. Canned broths may also be refrigerated, then skimmed of surface fat.

Chiles: There are many wonderful fresh and dried varieties available. They can liven up a low-fat dish by adding both flavor and color. The seeds and veins contain the most heat. Leave them in or remove them according to your own tolerance for spiciness.

Coarse or kosher salt: The coarser grain adds texture to food and brings the flavor up from its usual supporting role. It's wonderful on roasted vegetables and in salads.

Filo dough: Whenever possible, buy fresh filo sheets from a Middle Eastern or Greek market. Filo is also available in the freezer section of most grocery stores, but many times the packages will have sheets that are stuck together from the moisture of freezing and thawing. These frozen sheets tend to tear easily.

Flavored oils: Highly flavored oils, including sesame, mustard, garlic, herb-flavored oils and nut-flavored oils, can add a lot of flavor to a dish with a minimum of fat.

Herbs: Fresh are preferable to dried whenever possible. A few of my favorites are basil, for its pungent flavor that can punch up many low-fat dishes; dill, for its subtle flavor that works well in seafood and poultry recipes; and sorrel, an herb used commonly in European cooking that is becoming more common here. Sorrel's leaves resemble spinach and it has a pleasant tang.

Kefir: A cultured low-fat milk product that looks a bit like liquid yogurt and has the same tang as yogurt. It comes in several flavors, though plain is best for cooking. A cup of low-fat kefir contains 4.5 grams of fat. It is available in health food stores and specialty markets.

Milk: Milk labels have changed recently. Here's what to look for.

Fat-free milk: Has had as much fat removed as is technologically possible. Fat content is less than 0.25 percent.

Low-fat milk: Was recently reduced from 2 percent fat to 1 percent fat. It has 2.5 grams of fat per cup.

Reduced-fat milk: The former low-fat milk. It has 2 percent fat and 5 grams of fat per cup.

Whole milk: One cup of whole milk is 12 percent fat and contains contains 8 grams of fat per cup. Note that 1 tablespoon of whipping cream has 5 grams fat (which means 1 cup of whipping cream has 128 grams of fat).

Nonfat evaporated skim milk: Concentrated skim milk fortified with Vitamins A and D. It contains up to 0.5 percent milkfat; regular evaporated milk contains 1 gram of fat per tablespoon.

Mirin: A sweetened white rice wine available in Japanese markets.

Nonfat cottage cheese: Compare it to regular creamed cottage cheese, which contains has 4.75 grams of fat per 1/2 cup. To meet U.S. Department of Agriculture guidelines, "nonfat" cottage cheese may contain no more than .5 grams of fat per 1/2 cup.

Nonfat egg substitute: This contains 99 percent egg white and can be used in place of whole eggs in many recipes. Egg substitute contains no fat or cholesterol; a whole egg contains 5.6 grams of fat. Note that 1/4 cup is equivalent to 1 whole egg.

Nonfat sour cream: A good nonfat replacement for regular sour cream, which has 3 grams of fat per tablespoon.

Nonfat yogurt: Its tangy flavor works well in place of its higher-fat counterparts; a cup of regular plain yogurt contains 8 grams of fat compared to .5 grams in nonfat yogurt. It can also be substituted for sour cream in many instances.

Nonstick cooking spray: These commercial sprays come in basic oil flavors: Canola, olive and butter are common. The mesquite-flavored spray is good for using on indoor stove-top grills and adds a smoky barbecue taste. Many people, however, prefer to use their own higher-quality oils in spray pump bottles and mister bottles that are now on the market.

Pasta: Look for pastas made without egg for the lowest fat. A 2-ounce portion of dried pasta is a healthful serving when sauced with low-fat ingredients. Note that orzo is a tiny rice-shaped pasta used in making soups and salads.

Quinoa: The high-protein South American grain is becoming more popular here. It should be rinsed under cold water before cooking. And it's quick to make; it takes only about 10 minutes to cook. You know it's done when the grains turn translucent. Buy it in health food stores and specialty markets.

Rapini or broccoli rabe: Also known as "bitter broccoli," it's a wonderful alternative to the usual broccoli-on-the-side rut. Try sautéing it with garlic, then squeezing a bit of lemon juice on top before serving.

Rice and grains: Whole grains and rice are used often in low-fat cooking because they contain little or no fat and are high in fiber. Try steaming some of the longer-cooking varieties of rice such as brown and wild rice; it's a no-fuss way to cook them, and the texture is perfect.

Potsticker wrappers: Small rounds of wonton dough wrappers are used for making soup dumplings and are available in Asian groceries and supermarkets.

Soybeans: The high-protein legumes used to make tofu and other soy products. They are delicious fresh and can often be found at farmers markets and Asian markets. They are readily available dried.

Spring roll wrappers: They are thinner than the more familiar egg roll wrappers and are available in the freezer section of Chinese and Vietnamese markets and some supermarkets.

Tahineh: This sesame seed paste is not low-fat, but it can add a lot of flavor to food when used judiciously. It's most commonly used to make the Middle Eastern dip hummus and is available in Middle Eastern and specialty markets. When the jar is first opened, the oil is usually separated on the top; mix well before measuring. Keep it refrigerated once opened; it can become rancid quickly.

Tofu: Also called bean curd, it may be sold packed in water, in bulk or vacuum-packed. The vacuum-packed or silken tofu is usually found in the produce section of supermarkets. Tofu comes in a variety of consistencies: extra firm, firm, medium and soft. The firm varieties are best for stir-frying and crumbling over the top of dishes like cheese. Medium is best for casseroles, soups and salads. The softer ones are ideal for sauces, dips and drinks, for any time you don't need the tofu to hold its shape during cooking. Low-fat tofu has less than half the fat of regular tofu.

Vinegar: Herb vinegars such as dill, tarragon or rosemary are ideal flavor enhancements in low-fat cooking. Mild and slightly sweet rice vinegar is used in Asian cooking. And balsamic vinegar, a sweet aged Italian vinegar, is used often these days in low-fat cooking. Balsamic is good when used in dressings for salads and in marinades. When reduced, it takes on a syrupy consistency which is great when served as a sauce. Avoid using the highest grade balsamics for dressings, marinades and in food that will be cooked; the very best vinegars should be used only when they will be the star of the dish.

Equipment for the Low-Fat Kitchen

Cheesecloth: This works well to wrap fish for poaching and other delicate items; the cheesecloth helps items hold their shape during cooking. It's also useful for wrapping spices, mixed herbs or other items that need to be pulled out of a pot after cooking.

Egg separator: A small cup-like gadget with a slit in the bottom that fits on top of measuring cups and small bowls. When the egg is cracked into the cup, the yolk is easily separated from the white.

Gravy separator: It looks like a measuring cup with a spout that allows the fat to rise to the top so it can be poured off.

Grill pan: This is used for a quick, low-fat way to grill foods on a stove-top burner while giving an outdoor barbecue flavor to foods. It's best to buy a heavy cast-iron grill with ridges. The ridges act to elevate food out of the fat during cooking. Most pans have a little spout on the side to pour off excess fat. This type of grill pan, like any cast-iron pan, should be seasoned before you use it the first time. Clean the pan well, then cover the cooking surface generously with oil. Put the pan over low heat and allow it to heat 10 to 15 minutes, then wipe off the excess oil. After seasoning, rinse the pan under hot water after each use and do not use soap. Little or no oil should be needed once the pan is well-seasoned.

Mandoline: The hand slicer is used for cutting vegetables into assorted uniform sizes and shapes. It's good for slicing paper-thin vegetables.

Mortar and pestle: Instead of using an electric grinder, I prefer pounding spices and herbs with what might be among the world's oldest kitchen gadgets. I can control the coarseness better, and it doesn't take that much longer to use.

Nonstick pans: Buy the best-quality nonstick cookware in several sizes. The cheapest pans can quickly loose their coating. When using Teflon-coated pans (or a well-seasoned cast iron skillet) only a minimum of oil or nonstick cooking spray is necessary.

Oil misters or spray pump bottles: Oil misters, which are new on the market, allow you to put your own oil in the the mister and lightly spray skillets and cooking utensils. You can also fill a spray pump bottle with your favorite oil. You can use that pricey Tuscan extra-virgin olive oil—and you can go through the bottle *slowly*. A good alternative to commercial cooking sprays.

Parchment paper: This is used to line pans for fat-free baking. Foods such as chicken, fish and seafood can be sealed in parchment paper and baked.

Potato ricer: The ricer looks like a big garlic press. Cooked potatoes are put into the basket and pressed through. The result: lump-free mashed potatoes that are light and fluffy and not sticky or gluey from overmixing. The ricer is also good for other root vegetables and squash.

Rotisserie: A spit-roaster that slowly rotates to allow meat to "self-baste" as it turns and lets fat drip off as it cooks. Many ovens and barbecues have built-in rotisseries. There are also free-standing electric rotisserie units that can be used on a kitchen counter or the patio.

Sharp knives: A good set of knives that are well taken care of can last a lifetime. The sharper the knife, the easier your work will be.

Spiral cutter: A cutting gadget with blades that will cut vegetables into wide ribbons or thin noodle-like strands. It's great for cutting vegetables into attractive garnishes or just making a fun salad for yourself.

Steamer: There are several electric steamers on the market. You can also use the small fold-up steamer baskets that fit into most saucepans. Chinese bamboo steamers that fit on top of a wok filled with water are another option. Deep roasting pans are also great for steaming. Put a rack in the bottom and add water to just below the rack so the water doesn't touch the food. If you don't have a cover, use foil to cover the top.

Wok: A large wok with deep sides is best for stir-frying. For optimum results, heat the wok before adding oil. If you're using commercial cooking sprays, remove the wok from the heat before spraying to avoid flare ups. Like the grill pan, a wok is most useful for low-fat cooking when it is well-seasoned (see grill pan entry). After stir-frying, rinse the wok in hot water. Then, heat it for a minute or so on top of the stove to thoroughly dry it to prevent rusting.

Yogurt strainer: This fine mesh strainer is used to drain yogurt to a thick creamy consistency. The yogurt is left to drain in the refrigerator several hours or overnight until the right consistency is reached. The thickened yogurt can be used in place of high-fat cream cheese, sour cream and mayonnaise in many recipes for dips, salad dressings, cheesecakes, salads and other baked items.

Zester: A small gadget used to make thin strips of citrus peel for use in garnishing and cooking. It is most frequently used on limes, lemons and oranges. Care is needed to cut only into the colored surface of the fruit and not into the bitter white pith of the fruit.

COOKING TECHNIQUES OF THE LOW-FAT KITCHEN

Broiling: This direct-heat method of cooking is great for low-fat cooking. The food is cooked directly under the heating implement and placed on a rack over a drip pan to allow the fat to collect away from the food during cooking.

Dry frying: Many foods can be fried with little or no oil in a hot nonstick or well-seasoned cast-iron skillet with no oil. The food should brown quickly without drying out or sticking. Sliced eggplant, for instance, is terrific cooked this way.

Grilling: Indoors or outdoors, it's an excellent way to cook meats, poultry and fish with a minimum of added fat. If using a seasoned cast-iron grill, only a light mist of olive or canola oil or a commercial nonstick cooking spray is needed. Spray outdoor grills with nonstick cooking spray before starting up the flame to prevent sticking.

Microwaving: This is a quick and easy method of low-fat cooking and heating without the addition of fat.

Oven frying: Many foods that are traditionally deep-fried taste great prepared in an oven. The foods can be dipped in batter or bread crumbs (nonfat egg substitute is terrific for helping bread crumbs stick) then baked at a high temperature for maximum crunchiness. You'll find foods made this way have a crisp, clean flavor that deep-fried foods often lack.

Poaching: A common low-fat cooking technique in which food is cooked in a barely simmering liquid. To get the most flavor out of this method, add fresh herbs to the broth. And to keep the fat to a minimum, use low-fat or defatted chicken broths, beef broths and fish stocks. For desserts, try poaching fruit in simple syrup.

Roasting: A dry-heat method in which tender cuts of meat are cooked on a rack uncovered in the oven. For the lowest-fat roasting of meats, it's best to use a rack to lift the meat out of any fat that may collect in the bottom of the roaster. This also allows the heat to circulate around the entire roast for more even cooking.

Rotisserie cooking: An indirect-heat method of cooking in which food cooks on a spit that slowly rotates, allowing fat to drip off as it cooks. It's an especially good technique for cooking whole chickens and roasts.

Steaming: This moist-heat method of cooking preserves many of the nutrients and natural juices of foods. It is an especially good method for cooking vegetables, poultry and fish; fat tends to drip off meat during the cooking process. Steaming is also an excellent method for reheating foods so they won't dry out. The simplest way to steam is to place a rack over simmering water filled to at least 1 inch below the rack level. The food is placed on the rack, then covered and left to steam until cooked through.

Stir-frying: Cooking in a hot wok with a minimum of oil can give food a crisp exterior and tender interior. See wok information in Equipment section for more details.

[Breakfast and Brunch]

POTATO FRITTATA

- 1 POUND RED BOILING POTATOES
- 1/2 CUP MINCED ONION
- 2 CLOVES GARLIC, MINCED
- NONSTICK OLIVE OIL COOKING SPRAY
- 1 1/2 CUPS NONFAT EGG SUBSTITUTE (EQUIVALENT TO 6 EGGS)
- 2 TABLESPOONS CHOPPED CILANTRO
- 2 TABLESPOONS MINCED GREEN ONION
- SALT, PEPPER
- 2 TABLESPOONS CHOPPED TOMATO

Steam potatoes in steamer over boiling water until fork-tender, 30 to 35 minutes. Let cool long enough to handle and cut into 1-inch pieces.

Sauté potatoes, onion and garlic in 10-inch skillet sprayed with nonstick olive oil cooking spray over medium-low heat, stirring occasionally, until potatoes are browned, about 10 minutes.

Combine egg substitute, 1 tablespoon cilantro, 1 tablespoon green onion and salt and pepper to taste. Pour evenly over potatoes in skillet. Cover and cook over medium-low heat until eggs are set, 7 to 10 minutes. As frittata cooks, occasionally loosen edges with spatula and move around to prevent sticking.

When eggs are set, sprinkle with remaining cilantro and green onion and slide out of skillet onto serving plate. Garnish with chopped tomato.

6 servings. Each serving: 112 calories; 107 mg sodium; 0 mg cholesterol; .11 gram fat; 20 grams carbohydrates; 8 grams protein; 1.88 grams fiber.

Frittatas are terrific for brunch or as the main course for a light warm-weather dinner.

After adding the egg substitute, keep an eye on the frittata so that it doesn't brown too quickly on the bottom during cooking. Fresh seasonal fruit and a dollop of fresh goat's milk yogurt would make a great finishing touch.

BREAKFAST AND BRUNCH

Polenta makes great pancakes, slightly crunchy with the comforting flavor of corn. A hint of rosemary in the blackberry syrup adds a lovely herbal scent to the dish that is balanced nicely with a dollop of nonfat sour cream. When cooking the pancakes, resist the temptation to press them down with a spatula; it just makes them compact.

For best results, use regular polenta, not the instant variety.

POLENTA PANCAKES WITH SOUR CREAM AND BLACKBERRY SYRUP

BLACKBERRY SYRUP

1 1/2 TABLESPOONS CORNSTARCH

1/4 CUP SUGAR

1 CUP BLACKBERRY JUICE

1/2 PINT BLACKBERRIES

1 TABLESPOON MINCED ROSEMARY

PANCAKES

1 CUP CAKE FLOUR

1 CUP POLENTA

4 TEASPOONS SUGAR

2 TEASPOONS BAKING POWDER

1/2 TEASPOON BAKING SODA

1 TEASPOON SALT

2 CUPS BUTTERMILK

2 EGG WHITES

Nonstick cooking spray, optional

1 CUP NONFAT SOUR CREAM, OPTIONAL

BLACKBERRY SYRUP

Stir together cornstarch and sugar in small saucepan. Gradually blend in blackberry juice. Heat to boiling, stirring constantly. Stir in blackberries. Heat and stir, mashing some of blackberries with back of spoon. Stir in rosemary. Makes about 1 1/4 cups.

PANCAKES

Combine cake flour, polenta, sugar, baking powder, baking soda and salt. Stir in buttermilk just until blended. Beat egg whites until stiff but not dry. Fold into batter until just blended.

Heat skillet over medium-low heat until drop of water sizzles. Pour about 1/4 cup pancake batter onto nonstick griddle, well-seasoned skillet or skillet sprayed with nonstick cooking spray. Cook until pancake is puffed and dry around edges. Turn and brown other side. Serve hot with blackberry syrup and sour cream.

12 pancakes. Each pancake with 1 1/2 tablespoons syrup: 150 calories; 332 mg sodium; 2 mg cholesterol; 1 gram fat; 31 grams carbohydrates; 5 grams protein; 0.6 gram fiber.

APPLE PANCAKES

POACHED APPLES

1 cup sugar
1 cup water
1 cinnamon stick
3 whole cloves
4 Granny Smith apples, cored, peeled and sliced into 1/2-inch cross-wise rings

PANCAKES

2 cups flour
2 tablespoons plus 1/4 cup sugar
2 teaspoons baking powder
1 teaspoon salt
1/2 teaspoon baking soda
2 cups buttermilk
1/4 cup nonfat egg substitute
2 egg whites
1 teaspoon vanilla extract
Nonstick cooking spray
4 teaspoons cinnamon
Maple syrup, optional

POACHED APPLES

Combine sugar, water, cinnamon stick and cloves in saucepan and bring to boil, stirring occasionally. Reduce heat and simmer 5 minutes to blend flavors.

Add few apple slices to syrup and simmer, covered, until tender, 7 to 10 minutes. Remove from syrup with slotted spoon and place in deep-sided baking dish. Repeat until all apples are cooked. Pour any remaining syrup over apple slices in baking dish. Let stand until cool and refrigerate, covered, overnight.

When ready to bake pancakes, remove apple slices from syrup and pat dry with paper towels. Cut apple rings in half.

PANCAKES

Combine flour, 2 tablespoons sugar, baking powder, salt and baking soda in mixing bowl.

Combine buttermilk and nonfat egg substitute and stir into dry ingredients.

Beat egg whites until soft peaks form and fold into batter. Stir in vanilla.

Spoon about 1/4 cup batter onto nonstick griddle, seasoned skillet or griddle sprayed with nonstick cooking spray. Put 2 Poached Apple pieces on top of batter and cook over medium heat until pancake is set, bubbly around edges and golden brown on bottom, about 2 minutes. Turn and brown other side, about 1 minute. Repeat until all batter is used.

Combine remaining 1/4 cup sugar and cinnamon and sprinkle on hot pancakes or drizzle with maple syrup if desired.

16 pancakes. Each pancake, with cinnamon-sugar but without syrup: 154 calories; 244 mg sodium; 1 mg cholesterol; 1 gram fat; 35 grams carbohydrates; 3 grams protein; 0.22 gram fiber.

Granny Smiths are great apples for poaching and hold up well in apple pancakes (some varieties turn mushy and fall apart when poached). The apples will be more flavorful if allowed to stand in the syrup overnight, but it's not necessary if you don't have the time.

BREAKFAST AND BRUNCH

Whole-grain brown rice, higher in fiber than milled white rice, makes a substantial drink when blended with milk, brown rice syrup for sweetness and hints of vanilla extract and almond extract for flavor.

Gluten-free organic brown rice syrup, available in health food stores, is similar to honey in consistency but doesn't have the overpowering flavor and isn't as sweet.

The basis for this flavorful low-fat breakfast drink is a vanilla-flavored milk-like soy beverage made from cooked soybeans, filtered water, honey and vanilla. You'll find it in most supermarkets and health food stores and some Asian markets. It's a great product to use in smoothies and also tastes good poured over cereal.

ALMOND BROWN RICE BREAKFAST DRINK

2 CUPS NONFAT MILK
1 CUP COOKED BASMATI BROWN RICE
1/4 CUP BROWN RICE SYRUP
1/2 TEASPOON VANILLA EXTRACT
1/4 TEASPOON ALMOND EXTRACT
3 TO 4 ICE CUBES
2 TEASPOONS CHOPPED TOASTED SLICED ALMONDS

Blend 1/2 cup milk and warm rice in blender on high until smooth. Blend in rice syrup, vanilla and almond extracts until smooth. Add remaining 1 1/2 cups milk. Blend in ice cubes until frothy. Pour into serving glasses and sprinkle toasted almonds over top of each glass.

2 servings. Each serving: 302 calories; 147 mg sodium; 5 mg cholesterol; 2 grams fat; 57 grams carbohydrates; 12 grams protein; 0.21 gram fiber.

BERRY BLAST

1 CUP VANILLA SOY BEVERAGE
1 BANANA
1/2 CUP RASPBERRIES
1 TABLESPOON HONEY
1/4 CUP FROZEN NONFAT YOGURT
2 SLICES KIWI FRUIT

Process vanilla soy beverage, banana, all but 2 raspberries, honey and frozen yogurt in blender until well mixed.

Pour into 2 glasses and garnish each with 1 slice kiwi and 1 raspberry.

2 servings. Each serving: 156 calories; 50 mg sodium; 0 cholesterol; 2 grams fat; 32 grams carbohydrates; 6 grams protein; 1.39 grams fiber.

[Appetizers]

OVEN-FRIED ZUCCHINI

4 ZUCCHINI (ABOUT 1 POUND)

1/4 CUP NONFAT EGG SUBSTITUTE

1/3 CUP ITALIAN-STYLE BREAD CRUMBS

NONSTICK BUTTER GARLIC COOKING SPRAY

SALT

1/4 CUP GRATED PARMESAN CHEESE

Cut each zucchini lengthwise into 4 strips. Dip zucchini strips into nonfat egg substitute, then roll in bread crumbs to coat. Arrange in single layer on baking sheet sprayed with cooking spray. Lightly spray zucchini strips with cooking spray. Bake at 450 degrees until browned and fork-tender, about 25 minutes. Lightly sprinkle with salt to taste and Parmesan.

4 servings. Each serving: 85 calories; 455 mg sodium; 5 mg cholesterol; 2 grams fat; 10 grams carbohydrates; 6 grams protein; 0.57 gram fiber.

You can achieve a flavor close to that of deep-fried zucchini strips by using nonfat egg substitute and bread crumbs as a batter, then baking the zucchini in the oven. There's a clean, nongreasy taste to the baked strips that you might like even better than the taste of deep-fried.

APPETIZERS

This is an ideal party appetizer. It's quick, easy to prepare and certain to please your guests.

The sauce can be made and the shrimp wrapped several hours ahead of time. Then, all you have to do is grill the shrimp for just a few minutes.

BASIL- AND PROSCIUTTO-WRAPPED SHRIMP

5 CLOVES GARLIC, MINCED
2 TABLESPOONS SOY SAUCE
1 TABLESPOON LEMON JUICE
2 TABLESPOONS MINCED GINGER ROOT
2 TABLESPOONS MINCED PLUM TOMATOES
1/2 TEASPOON SUGAR
1/2 CUP CLAM JUICE

1 TABLESPOON OIL
12 LARGE SHRIMP, PEELED AND DEVEINED
12 LARGE BASIL LEAVES
4 VERY THIN SLICES PROSCIUTTO, CUT LENGTHWISE INTO 3 PIECES
NONSTICK OLIVE OIL COOKING SPRAY

Combine 4 cloves minced garlic, soy sauce, lemon juice, ginger, tomatoes, sugar and clam juice to make dipping sauce. Set aside.

Combine oil and remaining 1 clove minced garlic. Add shrimp, tossing to coat.

Wrap 1 basil leaf around middle of each shrimp, then 1 strip prosciutto, pressing end to seal.

Heat heavy stove-top iron grill until very hot, spraying with nonstick olive oil-flavored cooking spray.

Grill shrimp until pink and cooked through, about 3 minutes, turning once. Serve with dipping sauce.

12 shrimp appetizers. Each appetizer, with dipping sauce: 26 calories; 215 mg sodium; 11 mg cholesterol; 1 gram fat; 1 gram carbohydrates; 2 grams protein; 0.06 gram fiber.

SPANAKOPITA

- 1 TABLESPOON OIL
- 1 CUP SLICED GREEN ONIONS
- 1/4 CUP SNIPPED DILL WEED
- 2 (10-OUNCE) PACKAGES FROZEN CHOPPED SPINACH, THAWED
- 1/2 CUP FLOUR
- 1 1/2 TEASPOONS SALT
- 3 CUPS NONFAT MILK
- 1 CUP NONFAT EGG SUBSTITUTE (EQUIVALENT TO 4 EGGS)
- 2 CUPS NONFAT COTTAGE CHEESE
- 1 CUP CRUMBLED FETA CHEESE
- 1/4 TEASPOON WHITE PEPPER
- 1/2 TEASPOON BAKING POWDER
- 9 SHEETS FILO DOUGH
- NONSTICK BUTTER-FLAVORED COOKING SPRAY
- 1 TABLESPOON BUTTER, MELTED

Heat oil in skillet. Add onions and dill and sauté until tender.

Squeeze excess water from spinach. Add to skillet and sauté until heated through. Keep warm while making cream sauce.

Combine flour and salt in mixing bowl. Add just enough milk to make thin paste, about 3/4 cup.

Put remaining milk in saucepan and bring to boil. Stir in flour-and-milk paste. Return to boil and cook, stirring constantly, until just thickened.

Mix small amount of boiling sauce into egg substitute to temper.

Add tempered egg substitute to saucepan. Heat and stir until slightly thickened. Stir in cottage and feta cheeses, white pepper and baking powder. Stir in spinach mixture.

Arrange 3 sheets filo dough, each sprayed with butter-flavored nonstick cooking spray, in 13x9-inch baking pan sprayed with butter-flavored nonstick cooking spray.

Spoon 1/2 of creamed spinach mixture into pan. Repeat with 3 more sheets sprayed filo and remaining creamed spinach. Trim off excess filo around edges.

Arrange 2 sheets filo dough on top spinach layer and spray each with butter-flavored nonstick cooking spray. Top with last sheet filo dough. Tuck all sides into dish. Brush top with butter.

Bake at 325 degrees until lightly browned on top, 45 to 60 minutes.

12 servings. Each serving: 173 calories; 674 mg sodium; 10 mg cholesterol; 4 grams fat; 21 grams carbohydrates; 13 grams protein; 0.52 gram fiber.

Spanakopita, or spinach pie, is one of the most delightful Greek uses of filo dough. Unfortunately, the traditional recipe has a heavy cream sauce and calls for brushing each sheet of filo with butter. Nonstick cooking spray is used for the filo, then a little real butter is brushed on the top layer of the pie for flavor, but even that can be eliminated.

The base for the spinach filling is a nonfat "cream" sauce—a light paste of flour and nonfat milk enriched with egg substitute.

You can use store-bought filo dough, but you'll get better results if you buy fresh filo from a Middle Eastern or Greek market rather than the frozen filo available at supermarkets.

APPETIZERS

Caviar may be an indulgence when it comes to your bank account, but not if you're counting fat grams; an ounce, if you can afford it, contains only 5 grams. And you won't need much to make these stuffed potatoes truly luxurious. This might be one of the simplest and most elegant party hors d'ouevres you can serve. The potatoes can be prepped for baking several hours ahead of time, then filled and baked shortly before serving.

CAVIAR-STUFFED POTATOES

12 SMALL BOILING POTATOES, ABOUT 1 1/2-INCHES IN DIAMETER
NONSTICK OLIVE OIL COOKING SPRAY
SALT
3 CLOVES GARLIC, MINCED
1 TABLESPOON PREPARED HORSERADISH, OR TO TASTE
1/4 CUP LOW-FAT SOUR CREAM
1 TABLESPOON RED SALMON ROE
1 TABLESPOON BLACK LUMPFISH CAVIAR
FRESH SPRIGS ROSEMARY, OPTIONAL

Scoop out centers of potatoes. Put finished ones in cold water to prevent them from turning dark while standing. Drain well and pat dry before roasting.

Spray glass pie plate with olive oil cooking spray and arrange potatoes in 1 layer in plate. Spray potatoes with cooking spray and sprinkle with salt to taste, then minced garlic.

Bake potatoes at 450 degrees until potatoes are fork tender, about 25 minutes. Cool slightly.

Spread 1/4 teaspoon horseradish or more to taste inside each potato. Spoon about 1 teaspoon sour cream into each potato. Return to oven and bake until sour cream glazes, about 5 minutes.

Top half of each potato with 1/2 teaspoon salmon roe and half with 1/2 teaspoon lumpfish caviar. Line serving platter with fresh rosemary sprigs to garnish.

12 appetizer servings. Each serving: 34 calories; 73 mg sodium; 8 mg cholesterol; 0 fat; 7 grams carbohydrates; 1 grams protein; 0.19 gram fiber.

BAKED EGGROLLS

DIPPING SAUCE
1/2 CUP PLUM SAUCE
1 TABLESPOON SOY SAUCE

EGGROLLS
1 1/2 TABLESPOONS SOY SAUCE
2 TEASPOONS CORNSTARCH
1 TABLESPOON WATER
1/2 TEASPOON SALT
1 1/2 TEASPOONS SESAME OIL
NONSTICK COOKING SPRAY
2 CLOVES GARLIC, MINCED
1 TABLESPOON MINCED GINGER ROOT
1/2 CUP MINCED GREEN ONIONS
4 SHIITAKE MUSHROOMS, DICED
1/2 POUND SHRIMP, PEELED, DEVEINED AND CHOPPED
1 CUP BEAN SPROUTS
1 CUP SHREDDED NAPPA CABBAGE
8 SPRING ROLL WRAPPERS
1 EGG WHITE, BEATEN
SESAME SEEDS

DIPPING SAUCE
Stir plum sauce with soy sauce.

EGGROLLS
Combine soy sauce and cornstarch until smooth, then stir in water, salt and sesame oil. Set glaze aside.

Spray wok with nonstick cooking spray. Heat and add garlic, ginger, green onions and mushrooms. Stir-fry until mushrooms are tender, 3 to 5 minutes. Stir in shrimp and cook just until shrimp begin to turn translucent, about 1 minute. Add bean sprouts and cabbage. Sauté about 2 minutes or until cabbage is wilted and sprouts are crisp-tender.

Pour glaze over ingredients in wok. Heat and stir just until vegetables are glazed.

Lay 1 spring roll wrapper on work surface. Spoon about 1/4 cup filling onto wrapper in 4-inch diagonal strip about 1/3 way between opposite corners of wrapper. Fold closest corner over filling. Fold both side corners of wrapper to center. Roll up tightly.

Place rolls on baking sheet, seam-side down. Brush with beaten egg white and sprinkle with few sesame seeds. Bake at 425 degrees until browned and crisp, 15 to 20 minutes. Cut each eggroll into 2 to 3 sections and serve with Dipping Sauce.

8 eggrolls. Each eggroll, without dipping sauce: 123 calories; 454 mg sodium; 46 mg cholesterol; 2 grams fat; 18 grams carbohydrates; 9 grams protein; 0.44 gram fiber.

APPETIZERS

Although these eggrolls are filled with traditional Chinese ingredients, they use spring roll wrappers and are baked, rather than fried. (Baking in the usual eggroll wrappers produces tough and not very crisp eggrolls.)

Spring roll wrappers are paper-thin and need to be handled gently or they may tear during rolling. Don't let the filled wrappers stand too long before baking or they will become soggy. They are best when baked immediately after filling and eaten right away.

You can get spring roll wrappers in Chinese and Vietnamese markets and many supermarkets.

Spoon tangy sorrel sauce over these couscous-stuffed grape leaves and you have dolmathes with attitude. Actually, serving sorrel sauce over stuffed grape leaves with a few boiled new potatoes is traditional in Central and Eastern Europe.

Sorrel is a lemony herb that will cook down to a creamy, almost fluffy sauce when sautéed. The tartness of sorrel leaves varies, so taste the sauce before you add sugar; it may not need much at all.

Fresh sorrel is available in farmers markets at a reasonable price, but in a pinch you can use spinach. (If you use spinach, add lemon juice for tartness. Also, it won't be necessary to add sugar to the sauce.)

COUSCOUS-STUFFED GRAPE LEAVES WITH SORREL SAUCE

GRAPE LEAVES

- Nonfat low-sodium chicken broth
- 1/2 (10-ounce) box couscous
- Nonstick olive oil cooking spray
- 2 cloves garlic, minced
- 1 cup minced brown mushrooms
- 1/2 cup minced carrot
- 1/4 cup minced green onion
- 1/4 cup toasted pine nuts
- 2 tablespoons minced dill
- 1 tablespoon fresh lemon juice
- Salt
- 1 (8-ounce) jar whole grape leaves

SORREL SAUCE

- 1 pound sorrel leaves or spinach leaves
- 1 tablespoon butter
- 1 tablespoon flour
- 1/2 cup nonfat milk
- 1 teaspoon salt
- 2 tablespoons sugar, or to taste

GRAPE LEAVES

Bring 1 1/4 cups chicken broth to boil. Stir in couscous. Cover and remove from heat. Let stand 5 minutes. Fluff with fork.

Spray wok or skillet with olive oil cooking spray. Add garlic, mushrooms and carrot and sauté until mushrooms are tender, 2 to 3 minutes. Stir into couscous along with green onion, pine nuts, dill and lemon juice. Season to taste with salt.

Rinse grape leaves. Place 1 leaf, shiny side down, on counter. Snip off stem end. Spoon 1 generous tablespoon couscous filling onto grape leaf. Fold stem end of leaf over filling, then fold sides to center and roll up. Repeat with remaining grape leaves and filling.

Spray grill with nonstick olive oil and sear stuffed grape leaves on top of grill until lightly charred on all sides. Lightly spray grape leaves with olive oil while cooking.

Line bottom of large pot with unstuffed grape leaves. Arrange browned stuffed grape leaves, seam side down, in pot. Add chicken broth or water to cover. Put inverted plate on top of grape leaves to hold them in place while simmering. Bring to simmer, cover and cook until tender, 35 to 45 minutes. Remove from heat. Let stand to cool to warm. Remove plate from pot. Carefully remove cooked grape leaves to platter for serving.

SORREL SAUCE

Wash sorrel and remove any tough stems. Coarsely chop leaves. Set aside.

Heat butter in large saucepan until melted. Blend in flour until smooth. Cook and stir until flour turns medium brown. Stir in chopped sorrel. Cook and stir until leaves wilt and turn brownish green in color, about 2 minutes. Stir in milk. Heat to simmering and stir until sauce thickens, about 2 to 3 minutes. Stir in salt and sugar to taste. To serve, spoon sorrel sauce over stuffed grape leaves.

32 stuffed grape leaves. Each grape leaf: 37 calories; 131 mg sodium; 1 mg cholesterol; 1 gram fat; 6 grams carbohydrates; 2 grams protein; 0.18 gram fiber.

ARTICHOKE PESTO

1/2 (8 1/2-OUNCE) CAN QUARTERED HEARTS OF ARTICHOKES

1 CUP BASIL LEAVES

1 CUP ITALIAN PARSLEY LEAVES

1/3 CUP GRATED PARMESAN CHEESE

1 TABLESPOON LEMON JUICE

4 CLOVES GARLIC

1 SERRANO CHILE, CUT IN HALF AND SEEDED

1 TABLESPOON OLIVE OIL, OPTIONAL

1/2 CUP RIPE OLIVES

FRESH SLICED VEGETABLES, SUCH AS CARROT STICKS, CELERY STICKS, JICAMA STICKS, RADISH ROSES, SWEET RED OR GREEN PEPPER STRIPS, BROCCOLI FLORETS OR CAULIFLOWER FLORETS, OPTIONAL

Drain artichokes and reserve liquid. Set aside.

Place basil, parsley, cheese, lemon juice, garlic, chile and olive oil in food processor or blender and purée. Add reserved artichokes and olives and process until mixture is blended but slightly chunky. Stir in enough reserved liquid from artichokes to make pesto thin enough for dipping, about 2 to 3 tablespoons.

Serve with fresh sliced vegetables.

1 1/4 cups pesto. Each tablespoon, without olive oil: 23 calories; 69 mg sodium; 1 mg cholesterol; 1 grams fat; 3 grams carbohydrates; 2 grams protein;
0.36 grams fiber.

Each tablespoon, with olive oil: 29 calories; 69 mg sodium; 1 mg cholesterol; 2 grams fat; 3 grams carbohydrates; 2 grams protein; 0.36 grams fiber.

APPETIZERS

This version of pesto is made with artichoke hearts, serrano chiles, olives, lemon juice and parsley. It's aromatic and flavorful but has almost no oil.

The recipe calls for one tablespoon of olive oil, which isn't a lot. But that can be omitted if you are looking for a nonfat dip. The liquid from the artichoke hearts is used to thin the sauce enough for dipping or tossing with pasta.

Serve the pesto with fresh vegetables when serving it as a dip.

APPETIZERS

Seared ahi tuna skewers work not only as appetizers but also as a light main course when served with steamed rice. Keep a close watch when grilling; tuna cooks quickly and becomes tough if it's overcooked. Remove the skewers from the grill when the center of the tuna is still slightly pink.

The tuna can be grilled on a stove-top grill pan or over charcoal or a gas grill. Soak the bamboo skewers in water for about 15 minutes if cooking over a flame to help prevent burning.

Mirin is a sweetened white rice wine available at Japanese markets and many supermarkets.

AHI TUNA BITES WITH WASABI DIPPING SAUCE

1/2 POUND AHI TUNA
2 TEASPOONS PLUS 1/4 CUP MIRIN
2 TEASPOONS PLUS 1/4 CUP LIGHT SOY SAUCE
1 TEASPOON PLUS 2 TABLESPOONS SUGAR
1 TEASPOON PLUS 2 TABLESPOONS LEMON JUICE
1 1/4 TEASPOONS GRATED GINGER ROOT
3/4 TEASPOON WASABI PASTE
12 (6-INCH) BAMBOO STICKS
NONSTICK OLIVE OIL COOKING SPRAY, OPTIONAL
BLACK SESAME SEEDS

Cut tuna into 1 1/2-inch pieces and place in shallow glass dish. Combine 2 teaspoons mirin, 2 teaspoons soy sauce, 1 teaspoon sugar, 1 teaspoon lemon juice and 1/4 teaspoon ginger. Pour mixture over tuna and stir to coat. Cover and marinate 30 minutes.

Combine remaining 1/4 cup mirin, 1/4 cup soy sauce, 2 tablespoons sugar, 2 tablespoons lemon juice, 1 teaspoon grated ginger and wasabi. Set aside until ready to serve.

Thread 1 piece tuna on each bamboo stick. Grill on hot, well-seasoned grill pan or grill pan sprayed with nonstick olive oil cooking spray, turning to cook all sides, until tuna is almost done but still pink in center, 2 to 3 minutes. Sprinkle sesame seeds over tuna just before removing from grill.

Serve sticks as appetizer with dipping sauce.

12 sticks. Each stick with dipping sauce: 40 calories; 102 mg sodium; 7 mg cholesterol; 1 gram fat; 3 grams carbohydrates; 5 grams protein; 0.01 gram fiber.

[Soups]

TURKEY SOUP WITH RAPINI, SQUASH AND RUTABAGA

1 CLOVE GARLIC, MINCED

1/2 CUP ONION, MINCED

NONSTICK OLIVE OIL COOKING SPRAY

6 CUPS DEFATTED LEFTOVER TURKEY BROTH OR NONFAT CHICKEN BROTH

2 CUPS CUBED BANANA SQUASH (ABOUT 1/2 POUND)

1 RUTABAGA, PEELED AND CUBED

4 CUPS CHOPPED RAPINI (ABOUT 1/2 BUNCH)

1 CUP DICED WHITE TURKEY MEAT

SALT, PEPPER

Sauté garlic and onion in 4-quart saucepan sprayed with cooking spray until tender, 2 to 3 minutes.

Stir in turkey broth and bring to boil. Add cubed squash and rutabaga. Bring to simmer and cook until vegetables are fork tender, 20 to 25 minutes. Stir in rapini and simmer 5 minutes. Stir in turkey and heat until hot through. Season to taste with salt and pepper.

6 servings. Each serving: 100 calories; 247 mg sodium; 20 mg cholesterol; 1 gram fat; 6 grams carbohydrates; 16 grams protein; 0.87 gram fiber.

Turkey soup is comfort food all year long. Any combination of vegetables works well, but squash, rutabaga and rapini are especially nice together. The rapini or broccoli rabe, also known as "bitter broccoli," tends to get more bitter the longer it cooks. After five minutes of simmering, it's on the mild side; cook it longer if you like a stronger flavor.

This light, refreshing Chinese dumpling soup is made with fat-free chicken broth and turkey dumplings instead of the usual high-fat pork dumplings.

Round potsticker wrappers, available in many supermarkets and Asian markets, are used as dumpling wrappers. Just spoon a small amount of ground turkey filling onto each wrapper, then lightly brush the edge with beaten egg before sealing to prevent dumplings from opening during simmering.

CHINESE DUMPLING SOUP

1/2 POUND GROUND TURKEY

1 TABLESPOON MINCED GREEN ONION

2 TEASPOONS SOY SAUCE

2 TEASPOONS RICE VINEGAR

2 TEASPOONS MINCED GINGER ROOT

1 TEASPOON CORNSTARCH

1/2 TEASPOON SALT

1 (10-OUNCE) PACKAGE ROUND POTSTICKER WRAPPERS

1 EGG, BEATEN

4 (14 1/2-OUNCE) CANS FAT-FREE CHICKEN BROTH

1 SMALL BUNCH BOK CHOY, CUT CROSSWISE INTO 1-INCH SLICES

4 FRESH SHIITAKE MUSHROOMS, SLICED

1 (2 1/4-INCH) PIECE GINGER ROOT, PEELED AND SLICED

1/4 TEASPOON SESAME OIL

CHOPPED CILANTRO

Combine ground turkey, green onion, soy sauce, rice vinegar, minced ginger, cornstarch and salt in bowl. Brush outer edge of potsticker wrapper with beaten egg. Spoon about 1 teaspoon turkey mixture onto center of wrapper. Fold wrapper in half. Press firmly to seal well. Pleat edge. Repeat until all filling is used.

Combine chicken broth, bok choy, mushrooms and ginger in large sauce pot. Heat to boiling. Reduce heat, cover and simmer 5 minutes. Add filled dumplings. Return to boil. Reduce heat, cover and simmer 5 to 10 minutes, until dumplings are cooked through. Stir in sesame oil. Spoon into serving bowls. Sprinkle with chopped cilantro.

6 servings with about 30 dumplings. Each serving: 107 calories; 1,147 mg sodium; 53 mg cholesterol; 3 grams fat; 9 grams carbohydrates; 12 grams protein; 0.41 gram fiber.

CALIFORNIA CHILE SOUP

TORTILLA STRIPS

Nonstick cooking spray

2 corn tortillas, cut into 1/4-inch strips

Salt

SOUP

2 dried California chiles

2 cloves garlic, minced

1/2 cup chopped onion

Nonstick cooking spray

6 cups nonfat chicken broth

2 stalks celery, sliced

1 (14 1/2-ounce) can whole tomatoes

1/2 teaspoon ground cumin

1 teaspoon Mexican oregano

1/4 cup cilantro leaves

1/4 cup masa harina (masa flour)

2 corn cobs or 4 mini frozen corn cobs (thawed if frozen), cut into 1-inch chunks

TORTILLA STRIPS

Spray 11x15-inch baking pan with nonstick cooking spray. Spread tortilla strips in single layer. Lightly spray strips with nonstick cooking spray. Lightly sprinkle with salt to taste. Bake strips at 425 degrees until lightly browned and crisp, 10 to 15 minutes.

SOUP

Heat chiles in hot skillet or on hot griddle, turning until warm and pliable, 1 minute. Remove stems and seeds and devein chiles. Soak chiles in warm water to cover until softened, about 30 minutes. Purée chiles in blender with 1/2 cup chile soaking water.

Sauté garlic and onion in large sauce pot sprayed with nonstick cooking spray until onion is tender, 1 to 2 minutes. Stir in puréed chiles and simmer about 10 minutes. Add chicken broth, celery, tomatoes with liquid, cumin, oregano and cilantro. Bring to boil, then reduce heat and simmer, covered, about 15 minutes to blend flavors.

Whisk together masa harina and 6 tablespoons cold water until smooth. Gradually stir into simmering liquid. Return to boil and simmer 1 minute.

Add corn and simmer additional 1 to 2 minutes until hot throughout. Serve topped with Tortilla Strips.

4 servings. Each serving, without Tortilla Strips: 94 calories; 973 mg sodium; 0 cholesterol; 2 grams fat; 15 grams carbohydrates; 5 grams protein; 1.09 grams fiber.

Each serving, with Tortilla Strips: 124 calories; 1,065 mg sodium; 0 cholesterol; 3 grams fat; 21 grams carbohydrates; 6 grams protein; 1.09 grams fiber.

Dried California chiles soaked in water and puréed give this soup an earthy flavor and a rich adobe color. Substitute vegetable broth for the chicken if you want to make it even lighter.

Masa flour is used to thicken the soup slightly, giving it a toasty corn tortilla flavor. Corn tortilla strips baked in the oven until crisp add crunch.

SOUPS

Borrowing an idea from Indian cuisine, I sauté lentils until they're crunchy, then sprinkle them over the top of this curried soup. Some people have told me they're better than croutons.

Fried lentils also make a great snack on their own and are much lower in fat than nuts.

The smaller orange sweet potatoes, not the larger, darker ones, are preferable for this recipe because they give the soup a brighter color.

CURRIED SWEET POTATO SOUP

LENTIL GARNISH
1/4 CUP LENTILS
NONSTICK COOKING SPRAY
1 TABLESPOON OIL
SALT

SOUP
2 POUNDS SMALL SWEET POTATOES
NONSTICK COOKING SPRAY
1 ONION, DICED
3 CLOVES GARLIC, MINCED
1 TABLESPOON CURRY POWDER
1 TEASPOON PAPRIKA
1/2 TEASPOON GROUND CUMIN
1 QUART NONFAT CHICKEN BROTH
CHOPPED CILANTRO

LENTIL GARNISH

Rinse lentils well under running water, then soak in bowl of water to cover overnight. Drain and pat dry on paper towels.

Spray wok or small skillet with nonstick cooking spray. Add oil and heat over low heat until hot. Add drained lentils and sauté until they are browned and crisp, about 30 minutes. Sprinkle with salt while frying. Drain on paper towels and pat off any excess oil with paper towels. Set aside.

SOUP

Roast potatoes in shallow baking pan at 400 degrees until fork-tender in center, about 1 hour, 15 minutes. Remove from oven and let stand few minutes until cool enough to handle. Quarter and remove skins.

Spray bottom and sides of skillet with nonstick cooking spray. Add onion and garlic and sauté until lightly browned. Stir in curry powder, paprika and cumin and continue to sauté 1 minute to bring out flavors. Stir in chicken broth. Bring to boil. Purée sweet potatoes in food processor or blender, adding hot broth until mixture is smooth. Serve sprinkled with Lentil Garnish and chopped cilantro.

6 (1-cup) servings with garnish. Each serving, with garnish: 243 calories; 451 mg sodium; 0 cholesterol; 3 grams fat; 48 grams carbohydrates; 6 grams protein; 2.11 grams fiber.

ESCAROLE CHICKEN SOUP

1 (1 1/2- TO 2-POUND) CHICKEN
2 (49 1/2-OUNCE) CANS NONFAT CHICKEN BROTH
1 CELERY TOP
1 SMALL ONION, QUARTERED
NONSTICK COOKING SPRAY
3 CLOVES GARLIC, MINCED
1 HEAD ESCAROLE, CUT INTO 1-INCH CROSSWISE SLICES
2 TABLESPOONS LEMON JUICE
LIME SLICES
CILANTRO SPRIGS

Wash chicken well and remove giblets. Save liver for another use and set aside remaining giblets.

Place whole chicken in soup pot along with chicken broth, celery top and onion. Add remaining giblets. Bring to boil. Reduce heat, cover and simmer until chicken is tender, 35 to 45 minutes. Remove chicken from broth and let cool. Chill chicken broth overnight separately from chicken or let broth stand until fat rises to top. Skim off excess fat and strain, discarding celery top and onion. Discard skin or reserve for another use. Cover meat and set aside.

Lightly spray wok or skillet with nonstick cooking spray. Add garlic and sauté lightly. Add escarole and cook, stirring, until tender, about 10 minutes. Add escarole to broth and heat to boiling. Stir in lemon juice.

Arrange several slices of chicken breast in bottom of large soup plate. Spoon broth over top. Garnish each with lime slice and cilantro sprig.

6 to 8 servings. Each of 8 servings: 137 calories; 136 mg sodium; 33 mg cholesterol; 8 grams fat; 4 grams carbohydrates; 12 grams protein; 0.17 grams fiber.

The slightly bitter flavor of escarole and the tartness of lemon juice give this chicken broth a light, clean taste. You get more flavor when you poach chicken in nonfat chicken broth instead of water. Be sure to skim excess fat off the broth before adding the escarole. Note that the fat count given here can be lowered significantly through diligent skimming. The figures here reflect standard skimming.

After having a version of this great-tasting Chinese soup in a Los Angeles Chinatown restaurant, I tried to recreate it. Nonfat chicken broth is simmered with garlic and ginger, then allowed to steep to develop more flavor.

To keep the fat count down, use low-fat tofu. And instead of stuffing the tofu—a more difficult technique—press the shrimp paste onto the outside of the tofu. Spreading a little cornstarch over the tofu just before pressing on the shrimp paste helps "glue" the mixture into place.

The broth "cooks" the lettuce enough to make it limp, yet leaves a slight crunch, which gives the soup a nice texture and flavor.

CHINESE VEGETABLE SOUP WITH TOFU

- 1 QUART NONFAT CHICKEN BROTH
- 2 CLOVES GARLIC, SLICED
- 4 SLICES GINGER ROOT, ABOUT 1/4-INCH THICK
- 1/4 POUND SHRIMP, PEELED AND MINCED (ABOUT 1/3 CUP)
- 1 TEASPOON MINCED GREEN ONION
- 1/2 TEASPOON MINCED GINGER ROOT
- 1/4 TEASPOON SALT
- 1/4 TEASPOON SESAME OIL
- 1 1/2 TEASPOONS CORNSTARCH PLUS EXTRA FOR DUSTING
- 1/2 EGG WHITE (ABOUT 1 TABLESPOON)
- 1 (10 1/2-OUNCE) BOX FIRM, LOW-FAT TOFU, DRAINED
- 1 (3.325-OUNCE) CAN STRAW MUSHROOMS, DRAINED, OR 4 OUNCES FRESH STRAW MUSHROOMS
- SEVERAL ICEBERG LETTUCE LEAVES
- GREEN ONION STRIPS
- CILANTRO LEAVES

Combine chicken broth, garlic and ginger in 4-quart saucepan. Bring to boil. Reduce heat, cover and simmer about 5 minutes to blend flavors. Remove from heat and let stand covered for few minutes while preparing tofu cubes.

Combine minced shrimp, minced green onion, minced ginger, salt, sesame oil, 1 1/2 teaspoons cornstarch and egg white.

Cut tofu into quarters. Cut each quarter piece in half. Sprinkle bit of cornstarch on top of each piece of tofu and, using your fingers, smooth cornstarch evenly over top. Spoon and pat shrimp mixture on top of each piece of tofu.

Strain broth and add mushrooms. Bring broth to simmer. Add shrimp tofu to broth and simmer just until shrimp is cooked, 5 to 7 minutes.

To serve, line bottom of serving bowl with lettuce leaves. Spoon hot broth and shrimp tofu over lettuce. Top with green onion strips and cilantro leaves.

2 servings. Each serving: 180 calories; 1,665 mg sodium; 75 mg cholesterol; 5 grams fat; 8 grams carbohydrates; 24 grams protein; 0.14 gram fiber.

SALMON CHOWDER

FISH STOCK

2 POUNDS FISH BONES
1 SMALL ONION, SLICED
1 QUART WATER
1 CUP DRY WHITE WINE
1 SMALL CELERY STALK
1/4 TEASPOON SALT
1/8 TEASPOON WHITE PEPPER

CHOWDER

1 (14 1/2-OUNCE) CAN NONFAT CHICKEN BROTH
2 LARGE RED BOILING POTATOES, PEELED AND DICED
3 TABLESPOONS FLOUR
3 TABLESPOONS WATER
1/2 POUND COHO SALMON FILLET
1 TABLESPOON MINCED FRESH DILL
1 TABLESPOON LEMON JUICE
SALT
WHITE PEPPER

FISH STOCK

Bring fish bones, onion, water, wine, celery, salt and white pepper to taste to boil in 4-quart saucepan. Reduce heat and simmer 15 minutes. Remove from heat and strain.

CHOWDER

Add chicken broth to Fish Stock in pot and return to boil. Add diced potatoes, cover and simmer until potatoes are tender, 15 to 20 minutes.

Blend together flour and water in bowl until smooth. Stir into boiling stock. Boil and stir until slightly thickened, 1 to 2 minutes.

Skin salmon fillet, cut crosswise into 1/2-inch strips and add to broth. Simmer over low heat until salmon is cooked through, 1 to 2 minutes. Gently stir in dill and lemon juice. Add salt and white pepper to taste.

6 servings. Each serving: 127 calories; 365 mg sodium; 19 mg cholesterol; 3 grams fat; 7 grams carbohydrates; 11 grams protein; 0.09 gram fiber.

SOUPS

The word "chowder" sparks images of rich, creamy soup. This chowder is rich and creamy-tasting, but it has just 3 grams of fat.

The broth is made from a fresh fish stock combined with a little nonfat chicken broth for richness. After the potatoes have cooked, the soup is thickened with a slurry of flour blended with water. Stir in the fresh dill and lemon juice gently so as not to break up the salmon.

[Salads]

Here are three classic salad dressings that have been treated to a low-fat makeover. Each contains less than one gram of fat per tablespoon and can be mixed and matched to your favorite salads.

NONFAT THOUSAND ISLAND DRESSING

- 2 HARD-BOILED EGG WHITES, CHOPPED
- 1 CUP NONFAT MAYONNAISE
- 1/4 CUP CHILE SAUCE
- 1 TABLESPOON DRAINED SWEET PICKLE RELISH
- 1 TABLESPOON MINCED GREEN ONION
- 1 SMALL CLOVE GARLIC, MINCED
- 1/4 TEASPOON CRACKED BLACK PEPPER
- 1 TO 2 TABLESPOONS NONFAT MILK

Combine egg whites, mayonnaise, chile sauce, pickle relish, onion, garlic and pepper in bowl. Stir in enough milk to thin to desired consistency.

About 1 1/2 cups. Each 1-tablespoon serving: 11 calories; 124 mg sodium; 0 cholesterol; 0 fat; 3 grams carbohydrates; 0 protein; 0.01 gram fiber.

NONFAT RANCH-STYLE DRESSING

- 1/2 CUP NONFAT SOUR CREAM
- 1/2 CUP NONFAT MAYONNAISE
- 1 CUP BUTTERMILK
- 1 TEASPOON GRATED ONION
- 2 CLOVES GARLIC, MINCED
- 1/4 TEASPOON DRIED OREGANO LEAVES, CRUSHED
- 1/4 TEASPOON DRIED BASIL LEAVES, CRUSHED
- 1/4 TEASPOON DRIED MARJORAM LEAVES, CRUSHED
- 1/2 TEASPOON SALT

Blend together sour cream and mayonnaise in bowl.

Stir in buttermilk until blended. Stir in onion, garlic, oregano leaves, basil leaves, marjoram leaves and salt. Chill until serving time.

2 cups. Each 1-tablespoon: 8 calories; 79 mg sodium; 0 cholesterol; 0 fat; 2 grams carbohydrates; 1 gram protein; 0 fiber.

NONFAT GREEN GODDESS DRESSING

- 1 CUP NONFAT MAYONNAISE
- 1 CUP PARSLEY, STEMS REMOVED
- 1/4 CUP CHOPPED GREEN ONION TOPS
- 2 TABLESPOONS ANCHOVY PASTE
- 2 TABLESPOONS TARRAGON VINEGAR
- JUICE OF 1/2 LEMON
- 2 CLOVES GARLIC
- FRESHLY GROUND PEPPER
- 1/2 CUP NONFAT MILK

Combine mayonnaise, parsley, onions, anchovy paste, vinegar, lemon juice, garlic, pepper and nonfat milk in blender. Process until smooth.

1 1/3 cups. Each 1-tablespoon serving: 13 calories; 114 mg sodium; 1 cholesterol; 0 fat; 3 grams carbohydrates; 0 protein; 0.08 gram fiber.

All three of these salad dressings may also be used as appetizer dips with fresh vegetables or toasted low-fat pita bread slices. They can also be used as spreads in sandwiches in place of the traditional mayonnaise or butter.

Orzo, the tiny, quick-cooking rice-shaped pasta, makes a good salad base. Juices from chopped vegetables, along with white wine, vinegar and fresh lemon juice form the no-oil dressing.

For an excellent variation on this recipe, substitute three cups of whole cooked medium shrimp for the turkey.

ORZO CHOPPED SALAD

2 TEASPOONS OLIVE OIL
1/2 CUP CHOPPED ONION
1 CUP ORZO
2 CUPS CHICKEN BROTH, FAT SKIMMED
1 BUNCH ASPARAGUS, TOUGH STEMS REMOVED
1/4 CUP WHITE WINE VINEGAR
2 TOMATOES, DICED

2 CUPS CILANTRO LEAVES, CHOPPED
2 TABLESPOONS LEMON JUICE
1 (1-POUND) PACKAGE BONELESS TURKEY BREAST CUTLETS, ABOUT 6
2 CLOVES GARLIC, MINCED
SALT, PEPPER
5 CUPS COARSELY CHOPPED ROMAINE LETTUCE

Heat oil in large saucepan, add onion and cook until translucent. Stir in orzo, then chicken broth. Bring to boil. Reduce heat and simmer until orzo is tender and broth is absorbed, 9 to 11 minutes.

Blanch asparagus in boiling water about 3 minutes. Cut into 1/2-inch pieces. Set aside.

Spoon orzo mixture into large bowl. Add vinegar and stir in gently to prevent orzo from sticking. Stir in tomatoes, asparagus, cilantro and lemon juice.

Rub turkey cutlets with minced garlic. Season to taste with salt and pepper. Grill on medium-hot grill until cutlets are cooked through, 5 to 10 minutes. Remove from grill and cut into strips. Stir into orzo mixture. Chill until ready to serve.

Stir romaine into orzo just before serving. Season to taste with salt and pepper.

12 (1-cup) servings. Each serving: 71 calories; 143 mg sodium;
16 mg cholesterol; 1 gram fat; 6 grams carbohydrates; 8 grams protein;
0.36 gram fiber.

DILLED POTATO AND HARICOTS VERTS SALAD

3 POUNDS RED BOILING POTATOES
1/2 CUP REDUCED-FAT MAYONNAISE
1/3 CUP NONFAT CHICKEN BROTH
1 TABLESPOON DIJON MUSTARD
1 TEASPOON LEMON JUICE
2 TABLESPOONS CHOPPED DILL
1 TEASPOON SALT
1/2 CUP CHOPPED RED ONION
1/4 POUND HARICOTS VERTS, TRIMMED
1 HEAD ROMAINE
SNIPPED CHIVES

Cook potatoes in boiling salted water to cover until tender but not mushy when pierced with fork, 25 to 30 minutes. Drain. Let potatoes stand just until cool enough to handle. Cut into 1 1/2-inch pieces.

Whisk together mayonnaise and chicken broth until blended. Stir in mustard, lemon juice, dill and salt. Lightly toss potatoes with onion. Add dressing and toss until potatoes are evenly coated.

Blanch haricots verts in boiling water about 2 minutes. Drain and immediately plunge into ice or very cold water until chilled. Drain well and cut in half crosswise. Stir into potato salad. Chill several hours or overnight.

To serve, spoon onto chilled romaine leaves and sprinkle with snipped chives.

5 1/2 cups or 11 servings. Each 1/2-cup serving: 137 calories; 319 mg sodium; 0 cholesterol; 4 grams fat; 23 grams carbohydrates; 3 grams protein; 0.74 gram fiber.

SALADS

The flavor of fresh dill brightens the mild flavors of this salad. Fresh haricots verts add color and crunch. If you can't find the thin French-style green beans, thicker green beans will work well too.

Potato salad is best when allowed to chill several hours in the refrigerator and tastes even better when refrigerated overnight.

SALADS

Often, eggplant slices are fried, and when they are, they absorb a great deal of oil. For this salad—almost a dip that works well with bruschetta—eggplant slices are roasted to bring out their smoky flavor. No extra oil is needed to dress the eggplant when you mix it with a roasted garlic purée.

ROASTED EGGPLANT SALAD

1 HEAD GARLIC
SALT
OLIVE OIL COOKING SPRAY
2 EGGPLANTS, CUT INTO 1-INCH SLICES
2 TABLESPOONS CHOPPED CILANTRO
2 TABLESPOONS MINCED GREEN ONIONS

2 TEASPOONS MINCED BASIL PLUS 2 BASIL LEAVES CUT CROSSWISE INTO THIN STRIPS
4 TEASPOONS BALSAMIC VINEGAR
2 TEASPOONS LEMON JUICE
1 SMALL TOMATO, CHOPPED
4 SLICES RUSTIC BREAD, TOASTED

Cut top quarter off garlic head. Place whole head on square of foil. Sprinkle with salt to taste and spray lightly with olive oil cooking spray. Fold edges of foil to seal. Set aside.

Arrange eggplant slices in single layer on baking sheets sprayed with olive oil cooking spray. Lightly spray eggplant with cooking spray. Place garlic packet on baking sheet with eggplant slices. Roast garlic and eggplant at 425 degrees until eggplant is tender and lightly browned and garlic is soft, about 25 minutes. Let cool to room temperature.

Remove peel from eggplant slices and break up into shreds or small pieces. Place in bowl and stir in cilantro, onions and 2 teaspoons minced basil.

Squeeze garlic from cooked cloves into separate small bowl and mash. Stir in vinegar, lemon juice and 1/2 teaspoon salt. Stir mixture into eggplant. Let eggplant chill in refrigerator at least 30 minutes to allow flavors to blend.

Spoon eggplant onto platter. Sprinkle chopped tomato around eggplant and sprinkle with basil strips. Serve with toasted bread.

4 servings. Each serving: 136 calories; 284 mg sodium; 1 mg cholesterol; 1 gram fat; 28 grams carbohydrates; 5 grams protein; 0.94 gram fiber.

BAJA SQUID SALAD

2 POUNDS SQUID, CLEANED
4 CLOVES GARLIC, CRUSHED
1/2 CUP CHOPPED RED ONION
3 PLUM TOMATOES, DICED
1 SMALL CUCUMBER, PEELED AND CHOPPED
1/4 CUP CHOPPED CILANTRO
2 TABLESPOONS LIME JUICE
1 SERRANO CHILE, CHOPPED
1 TEASPOON MEXICAN OREGANO
SALT
1 HEAD BUTTER LETTUCE

Cut cleaned squid crosswise into 1 1/2-inch pieces. Cook squid and tentacles in boiling salted water to cover just until edges begin to curl, 30 seconds to 1 minute. Drain and rinse under cold water.

Combine garlic, onion, tomatoes, cucumber, cilantro, lime juice, chile, oregano and salt to taste. Add squid and toss. Chill.

Arrange several leaves butter lettuce on each of 6 plates. Spoon salad onto lettuce and serve.

6 servings. Each serving: 99 calories; 91 mg sodium; 197 mg cholesterol; 1 gram fat; 7 grams carbohydrates; 14 grams protein; 0.56 gram fiber.

The major work in preparing squid is the cleaning. First, pull the head from the body, then remove the long, clear plastic-like quill from the inner body and rinse well under cold water. After scraping off the outer skin with a knife, rinse again under cold running water. Cut the tentacles off the head in one piece and push out the beak. The squid is then ready to cook. Be careful not to overcook the squid or it can quickly turn tough and chewy.

SHRIMP AND GARLIC COLESLAW

GARLIC SHRIMP
2 TABLESPOONS VINEGAR
1 TABLESPOON OIL
1 TEASPOON SALT
3 TO 4 CLOVES GARLIC, MINCED
1/2 POUND COOKED BAY SHRIMP

SLAW
1/2 HEAD CABBAGE, FINELY SHREDDED
1/4 RED ONION, THINLY SLICED
3 TABLESPOONS CHOPPED CILANTRO
1/2 CUCUMBER, PEELED, SEEDED AND SLICED
1 TOMATO, CHOPPED
2 TABLESPOONS LIME JUICE

GARLIC SHRIMP

Combine vinegar, oil, salt and garlic. Add shrimp and marinate 30 minutes.

SLAW

Combine cabbage, onion and cilantro. Add cucumber and tomato and toss. Add Garlic Shrimp and toss again. Drizzle with lime juice, toss and serve.

10 servings. Each 1/2-cup serving: 65 calories; 307 mg sodium; 44 mg cholesterol; 2 grams fat; 7 grams carbohydrates; 6 grams protein; 0.65 gram fiber.

To shave time off your preparation, marinate the shrimp in the dressing while preparing the remaining ingredients. The cabbage can be finely shredded in a food processor. For the crispest slaw, drench the shredded cabbage in ice water after shredding.

SALADS

The truth is, this is more of a vegetable salad than a conventional potato salad. Arugula adds texture and a nicely sharp flavor; cilantro brightens the vinaigrette and roasted peppers add smokiness.

The fastest way to roast a bell pepper is to hold it over a gas stove top burner with a long-handled barbecue fork. Or you can cook the pepper on a rack under a broiler, turning until all sides are charred, 10 or 15 minutes. When the pepper is completely softened and charred, put it into a paper bag or covered bowl and let it stand about 15 minutes to steam so the skin will slip off easily.

POTATO SALAD WITH CILANTRO VINAIGRETTE

2 1/2 pounds red boiling potatoes, cut into 2-inch pieces

Nonstick olive oil cooking spray

3 cloves garlic, minced

Salt

Cracked black pepper

1 yellow bell pepper, roasted, peeled, cored, seeded and diced

1 cup chopped green onions

3 tomatoes, cut into 1-inch cubes

1/4 cup rice vinegar

1 tablespoon sugar

2 teaspoons olive oil

1/2 cup nonfat chicken broth

1/2 teaspoon lemon juice

1 cup cilantro leaves, chopped

1 bunch arugula

Spray both potatoes and interior of 15x10-inch jelly roll pan with cooking spray. Sprinkle garlic over potatoes and season to taste with salt and cracked black pepper.

Arrange potatoes in single layer in jelly roll pan.

Roast at 475 degrees until fork tender and well browned, about 40 minutes. Turn with spatula several times during cooking to prevent sticking. Let cool to room temperature and transfer to bowl.

Add bell pepper, onions and tomatoes and toss together.

Combine vinegar, sugar, olive oil, broth and lemon juice. Stir in cilantro and pour dressing over vegetables and toss. Remove any tough stems from arugula, break up large leaves and stir into salad.

9 cups. Each 1-cup serving: 130 calories; 56 mg sodium; 0 cholesterol; 1 gram fat; 27 grams carbohydrates; 4 grams protein; 0.90 gram fiber.

FRESH VEGETABLE TOSS WITH WASABI VINAIGRETTE

CRISP WON TONS
4 WON TON WRAPPERS, CUT INTO THIN STRIPS
NONSTICK COOKING SPRAY
SALT

WASABI DRESSING
1/2 CUP LEMON JUICE
2 TABLESPOONS SOY SAUCE
2 CLOVES GARLIC, CRUSHED
1 TEASPOON WASABI PASTE
1 TEASPOON SUGAR
1/4 TEASPOON SALT

SALAD
1/2 DAIKON
2 CARROTS
24 CHINESE PEA PODS, CUT INTO JULIENNE STRIPS
3 GREEN ONIONS, SLICED DIAGONALLY
1/4 (4-OUNCE) BOX SPICY RADISH CLOVER

CRISP WON TONS
Arrange won ton strips on a large flat baking sheet sprayed with nonstick cooking spray. Lightly spray won ton strips with nonstick cooking spray. Lightly sprinkle with salt to taste. Bake at 400 degrees until won tons are lightly browned, 5 to 8 minutes.

WASABI DRESSING
Stir together lemon juice, soy sauce, garlic, wasabi paste, sugar and salt.

SALAD
Peel daikon and make thin, lengthwise slices with mandoline. Peel carrots, cut into 3-inch lengths and shred. Put each in a separate bowl with ice water to cover.

Just before serving, drain daikon and carrots. Toss together carrots, pea pods, onions and radish clover. Arrange daikon on plate. Top with tossed vegetables. Sprinkle Crisp Won Tons over the top of the salad. Serve with Wasabi Dressing.

2 servings. Each serving: 152 calories; 1,530 mg sodium; 1 mg cholesterol; 1 gram fat; 33 grams carbohydrates; 7 grams protein; 3.50 grams fiber.

A simple salad of daikon, carrots, pea pods, onions and radish clover is exactly right with an Asian-style vinaigrette of lemon, soy and a kick of wasabi paste. Won ton strips add an extra touch of crispness. If you like the jolt of wasabi, increase the amount of paste in the dressing to your own taste.

SHRIMP AND ARTICHOKE QUINOA SALAD

Quinoa is the base for this high-protein, low-fat seafood salad. It's easy to fix and can be prepared in less than half an hour. Don't forget to rinse the quinoa under cold water before cooking to remove the soapy flavors inherent in the grain.

Quinoa, grown in the Andean valleys of South America, is one of the world's most beautifully colored grains. It takes about 10 minutes to cook in boiling water; it's ready when the grains turn translucent.

LEMON VINAIGRETTE
- 1/3 cup lemon juice
- 1/4 cup chicken broth
- 1 tablespoon olive oil
- 1 tablespoon capers
- 2 teaspoons Dijon mustard
- 1 clove garlic, minced
- 1 teaspoon salt
- Cracked black pepper

SALAD
- 1 cup quinoa
- Water
- Nonstick cooking spray
- 1 (13 3/4-ounce) can quartered artichoke hearts in water, drained
- 2 cloves garlic, minced
- 1/2 pound shrimp, peeled, deveined and cut in half lengthwise
- 3 green onions, sliced diagonally
- 2 stalks celery, sliced diagonally
- 3 Roma tomatoes, chopped
- 1/4 cup chopped cilantro

SHRIMP GARNISH
- 24 shrimp in shell
- Mesquite-flavored nonstick cooking spray
- Salt
- Romaine lettuce

LEMON VINAIGRETTE

Whisk together lemon juice, broth, olive oil, capers, Dijon mustard, garlic, salt and pepper to taste.

SALAD

Rinse quinoa in bowl under cold running water. Drain.

Combine quinoa and 2 cups water in medium saucepan. Bring to boil. Reduce heat to simmer, cover and cook until water is absorbed and grains look translucent, 10 to 15 minutes.

Heat wok and spray with nonstick cooking spray. Add artichoke hearts and stir-fry until edges begin to brown, 3 to 4 minutes. Add garlic and continue to stir-fry until artichoke hearts are browned and garlic is cooked. Spray with additional cooking spray as needed during stir-frying. Add shrimp and stir-fry until opaque and cooked through, 2 to 3 minutes.

Add shrimp mixture to cooked quinoa. Stir in onions, celery, tomatoes and cilantro.

Pour Lemon Vinaigrette over salad and stir lightly just until evenly mixed. Chill until serving time.

SHRIMP GARNISH

Grill shrimp in shell on grill pan sprayed with mesquite-flavored cooking spray until shells turn bright red and shrimp are opaque, about 5 minutes. Lightly spray shrimp with cooking spray and sprinkle with salt while grilling.

Serve salad on romaine and garnish salad plates with grilled shrimp.

6 servings. Each serving: 224 calories; 832 mg sodium; 78 mg cholesterol; 5 grams fat; 28 grams carbohydrates; 16 grams protein; 2.67 grams fiber.

BLACK-EYED PEAS AND MUSTARD GREENS

- 1 (11-OUNCE) PACKAGE FRESH BLACK-EYED PEAS
- 3 CLOVES GARLIC, MINCED
- 1/3 CUP MINCED ONION
- 1 TOMATO, CHOPPED
- 1/4 CUP MINCED CILANTRO
- 2 TEASPOONS CHOPPED OREGANO
- 2 TABLESPOONS LEMON JUICE
- 1 TABLESPOON OLIVE OIL
- 1 1/2 TEASPOONS SALT
- 1/4 TEASPOON CAYENNE PEPPER
- 2 BUNCHES MUSTARD GREENS, STEMS REMOVED

Rinse black-eyed peas. Bring to boil with water to cover in saucepan. Reduce heat, cover and simmer until tender, 15 to 18 minutes. Drain.

Combine peas, garlic, onion, tomato, cilantro, oregano, lemon juice, oil, salt and cayenne in bowl.

Put 1 bunch mustard greens in steamer and steam about 10 minutes. Remove leaves from steamer and let cool enough to handle.

Chop cooked greens and stir into black-eyed peas. Cover and refrigerate several hours or overnight.

Just before serving, arrange leaves of remaining bunch mustard greens on platter and top with black-eyed peas.

6 servings. Each serving: 246 calories; 636 mg sodium; 0 cholesterol; 3 grams fat; 42 grams carbohydrates; 16 grams protein; 3.58 grams fiber.

Black-eyed pea dishes usually depend on pork for flavor. This salad gets its kick from garlic, herbs and cayenne pepper.

Fresh black-eyed peas can be found in the produce section of most markets and are convenient because there's no need for soaking or long cooking; they cook in less than 20 minutes.

For the best flavor, allow the salad to refrigerate overnight.

Kefir, a rich-tasting, low-fat cousin of yogurt, is the base for the mixed herb dressing in this garden vegetable salad. It can be found in the dairy section of many grocery stores and ethnic markets.

Kidney beans thicken the dressing and give it a creamy consistency. Zucchini, yellow squash, carrot and spinach make up the salad, but any fresh vegetables you have on hand can be used.

FRESH GARDEN VEGETABLE SALAD WITH MIXED HERB DRESSING

MIXED HERB DRESSING

1 CUP KEFIR
1/4 CUP CHOPPED GREEN ONION
1/4 CUP CHOPPED PARSLEY
2 CLOVES GARLIC, CHOPPED
1 TABLESPOON MINCED DILL
1 TABLESPOON CHOPPED MINT
1 TABLESPOON LEMON JUICE
1 TEASPOON SALT
1 (15-OUNCE) CAN WHITE KIDNEY BEANS, DRAINED AND RINSED

SALAD

1/4 CUP SUNFLOWER SEEDS
SALT
1 EAR CORN
2 ZUCCHINI
2 YELLOW SQUASH
1 LARGE CARROT, SHREDDED
8 CUPS SLICED SPINACH LEAVES
1 TABLESPOON THINLY SLICED BASIL LEAVES

MIXED HERB DRESSING

Purée kefir, onion, parsley, garlic, dill, mint, lemon juice and salt in food processor or blender until smooth. Blend in beans until smooth. Chill until serving time.

SALAD

Toast sunflower seeds in small skillet until lightly browned; sprinkle with salt to taste. Cool on paper towel.

Blanch corn in boiling water to cover 2 minutes. Plunge into cold water to stop cooking.

Drain and cut kernels from cob. Shred 1 zucchini and 1 yellow squash. Toss together with corn, shredded carrot and spinach leaves.

Slice remaining zucchini and yellow squash and arrange in alternating pattern on platter. Top with salad mixture. Sprinkle with toasted sunflower seeds. Sprinkle fresh basil over chilled dressing and serve with salad.

8 servings. Each serving, with dressing: 175 calories; 587 mg sodium; 2 mg cholesterol; 6 grams fat; 25 grams carbohydrates; 10 grams protein; 2.61 grams fiber.

ROASTED BEET SALAD WITH PICKLED ONIONS

- 1 RED ONION
- 1/2 CUP RICE VINEGAR
- 1 TEASPOON BALSAMIC VINEGAR
- 1/4 CUP SUGAR
- 1/2 TEASPOON SALT
- 2 BUNCHES (ABOUT 1 3/4 POUNDS EACH) BEETS, WITH TOPS
- NONSTICK OLIVE OIL SPRAY
- 1 HEAD GARLIC
- SALT
- CRACKED BLACK PEPPER
- 1/4 YELLOW BELL PEPPER, MINCED

Peel onion and slice paper-thin. Combine rice vinegar, balsamic vinegar, sugar and salt in nonreactive bowl. Add sliced onion, then cover and refrigerate overnight.

Cut tops off beets, leaving about 2 inches of stem. Spray baking pan with nonstick olive oil spray. Add beets and whole head garlic. Lightly spray vegetables with olive oil spray, then lightly sprinkle with salt to taste. Roast at 450 degrees until beets are fork-tender, 45 to 60 minutes. Remove garlic after about 30 minutes of roasting (it should be soft and lightly browned).

Remove beets from oven and let stand until cool enough to handle, about 20 minutes. Cut beets into 1/2-inch slices.

Drain onion, reserving vinaigrette. Squeeze garlic out of cloves, coarsely chop, then add to vinaigrette. Set aside.

Remove large stems from beet greens. Cut leaves crosswise into 1-inch strips. Spray large wok or skillet with nonstick cooking spray, add greens and sauté just until tender, 4 to 5 minutes. Season to taste with salt and cracked pepper.

To serve, divide greens among serving plates. Top with beets and drained pickled onion. Drizzle roasted garlic vinaigrette over all. Garnish with yellow bell pepper.

4 servings. Each serving: 207 calories; 598 mg sodium; 0 cholesterol; 1 gram fat; 49 grams carbohydrates; 5 grams protein; 2.74 grams fiber.

Roasting beets at a high temperature is one way to use these beautiful but often difficult-to-prepare vegetables. It brings out the sweetness of the vegetable.

Don't buy beets without their tops. The greens are sautéed just before serving and tossed with the salad, which is delicious served with feta or farmer's cheese. The juices from pickled red onions are used for the nonfat roasted garlic dressing.

One timesaver: It's not necessary to peel the beets before eating if they're young or home-grown.

Cook the broccoli and carrots just until they are tender yet still crisp. They may be steamed, boiled in a minimum of water to prevent loss of nutrients or microwaved. After cooking, cool the vegetables quickly by first draining, then rinsing them under cold water. Then plunge the vegetables into a bowl of ice water. This will keep the vegetables crisp and the colors vibrant. Drain them just before tossing with the rice.

Let the salad chill a few hours to allow the flavor to develop fully. The salad is a great main course when served on a bed of mixed sprouts, such as alfalfa, lentil and mung bean.

BROWN RICE AND FRESH VEGETABLE SALAD

NONSTICK COOKING SPRAY
1/2 CUP MINCED ONION
1 1/2 CUPS BROWN RICE
1 QUART PLUS 1/4 TO 1/2 CUP NONFAT, LOW-SALT CHICKEN BROTH
1 POUND BUTTON MUSHROOMS, SLICED
1 (6-OUNCE) PACKAGE BROWN MUSHROOMS, SLICED
4 LARGE CLOVES GARLIC, MINCED
JUICE OF 1 LEMON
4 CUPS BROCCOLI FLORETS, COOKED AND DRAINED
8 MEDIUM CARROTS, PEELED, THINLY SLICED, COOKED AND DRAINED
1 EAR CORN, KERNELS REMOVED AND BLANCHED
4 GREEN ONIONS, SLICED
1 TABLESPOON MINCED FRESH THYME LEAVES
SALT
FRESHLY GROUND BLACK PEPPER
1 (10-OUNCE) CARTON MIXED SPROUT SALAD
1/4 CUP PINE NUTS, TOASTED

Lightly coat large saucepan with cooking spray. Add onion and sauté until tender. Stir in brown rice. Cook and stir to lightly toast rice. Stir in 1 quart chicken broth. Bring to boil. Reduce heat, cover and simmer until rice is tender, about 40 minutes. Spoon into large bowl and let cool while preparing remaining ingredients.

Coat large skillet or wok with cooking spray. Add mushrooms and garlic and sauté until tender. Stir in lemon juice. Add mixture to rice.

Stir cooked broccoli and carrots, corn, onions and thyme into rice. Season with salt and pepper to taste. Add enough of remaining chicken broth to make salad moist yet not soggy. Chill until ready to serve. Spoon onto fresh sprouts and sprinkle with pine nuts.

8 servings. Each serving: 230 calories; 381 mg sodium; 0 cholesterol; 5 grams fat; 42 grams carbohydrates; 10 grams protein; 2.47 grams fiber.

OVEN-FRIED CHICKEN SALAD

CHICKEN
1 POUND CHICKEN TENDERLOINS
2 LARGE CLOVES GARLIC, MINCED
1 TABLESPOON CHILI POWDER
1 TABLESPOON LEMON JUICE
1 TEASPOON GROUND CUMIN
1 TEASPOON MEXICAN OREGANO, CRUSHED
SALT, PEPPER
SOUTHWESTERN SEASONED OIL SPRAY

SOUTHWEST SALSA DRESSING
2 PLUM TOMATOES, CHOPPED
2 TABLESPOONS MINCED ONION
1 CLOVE GARLIC, MINCED
1 SERRANO CHILE, MINCED
2 TABLESPOONS MINCED CILANTRO
2 TABLESPOONS LIME JUICE
1 (5 1/2-OUNCE) CAN TOMATO JUICE
SALT

SALAD
3 HEADS BOSTON LETTUCE
1/2 (6-OUNCE) CARTON ALFALFA SPROUTS
1 (1-POUND) CAN PINTO BEANS, DRAINED
1/4 CUP SLICED GREEN ONIONS
4 SLICES LIME

CHICKEN
Combine chicken, garlic, chili powder, lemon juice, cumin, oregano and salt and pepper to taste in glass dish and marinate, covered in refrigerator, several hours. Just before ready to serve, spray large baking pan with Southwestern seasoned oil spray. Arrange marinated chicken tenderloins in single layer in pan. Bake at 500 degrees until browned and cooked through, about 5 minutes.

SOUTHWEST SALSA DRESSING
Combine tomatoes, onion, garlic, chile, cilantro and lime juice. Stir in tomato juice. Season to taste with salt. Purée half of mixture in food processor or blender. Combine purée and remaining tomato mixture. Refrigerate until serving time.

SALAD
Arrange some outer leaves of lettuce on serving plates. Chop remaining lettuce to measure 6 cups. Divide chopped lettuce and alfalfa sprouts among 6 chilled plates. Arrange chicken tenderloins on top of lettuce. Sprinkle beans and sliced green onions over all. Garnish each with lime slice. Pass Southwest Salsa Dressing separately.

4 servings. Each serving: 242 calories; 714 mg sodium; 60 mg cholesterol; 4 grams fat; 27 grams carbohydrates; 27 grams protein; 3.25 grams fiber.

How about this for guiltless "fried" chicken salad? Chicken tenderloins—the little strips between breasts and ribs—are coated in a spice mixture and then baked at 500 degrees to oven-fry without added fat. The high temperature quickly browns the meat while retaining its juiciness.

The chicken is sliced and served on greens with alfalfa sprouts, pinto beans and green onions.

SALADS

Fresh soybeans and fresh lima beans together make a wonderful summer salad. If you can't find fresh soybeans, they're sold frozen in most Japanese markets.

As the soybeans cook, check periodically to be sure they are covered with water. Also taste to check for doneness. Because they're being used in a salad, they should be tender yet firm enough to hold their shape.

FARMERS MARKET SALAD

1/2 POUND FRESH OR FROZEN SOYBEANS
1 POUND FRESH LIMA BEANS
1 RED ONION, MINCED
2 CLOVES GARLIC, MINCED
1 CUP CHOPPED CELERY
1/2 CUP CRUMBLED FETA CHEESE
1/4 CUP LEMON JUICE
1 (2-OUNCE) CAN ANCHOVIES, DRAINED AND MINCED
6 RIPE PLUM TOMATOES, DICED
1 BUNCH WATERCRESS
8 KALAMATA OLIVES

Cook soybeans in boiling water to cover until tender but still slightly firm, 30 to 35 minutes. Skim off any foam. Drain and rinse under cold water. Cool.

Rinse limas well, place in 2-quart saucepan and add water to cover. Bring to boil. Reduce heat and simmer 35 to 40 minutes. Skim off any foam. Drain and rinse under cold water. Cool.

Toss together cooked soybeans, lima beans, onion, garlic, celery, feta cheese, lemon juice, anchovies and tomatoes.

Remove tough stems from watercress and stir into salad. Chill until serving time. Spoon onto platter when ready to serve and garnish with Kalamata olives.

16 servings. Each serving: 81 calories; 222 mg sodium; 5 mg cholesterol; 3 grams fat; 509 grams carbohydrates; 6 grams protein; 1.13 grams fiber.

SHREDDED CHICKEN SALAD

1/3 EUROPEAN CUCUMBER

2 CUPS SHREDDED COOKED CHICKEN BREASTS, SKIN REMOVED, ABOUT 2 LARGE CHICKEN BREAST HALVES

3 CLOVES GARLIC, MINCED

1/4 TEASPOON MINCED GINGER ROOT

2 TABLESPOONS SOY SAUCE

3 TABLESPOONS RICE VINEGAR

1 TABLESPOON SUGAR

1 TABLESPOON RICE WINE

1/4 TEASPOON SESAME OIL

SALT

1/2 CUP CILANTRO LEAVES

Peel and seed cucumber, then cut into 1/2-inch pieces to make 1 cup. Toss together chicken and cucumber.

Combine garlic, ginger, soy sauce, vinegar, sugar, wine and sesame oil. Pour dressing over chicken and cucumbers and toss to coat. Let sit 15 minutes for flavors to blend.

Season with salt to taste and sprinkle with cilantro leaves.

4 servings. Each serving: 147 calories; 632 mg sodium; 60 mg cholesterol; 4 grams fat; 5 grams carbohydrates; 23 grams protein; 0.19 gram fiber.

Although any cooked chicken breast meat—poached, leftover or purchased in the deli section of your supermarket—will work in this simple Asian salad, steamed chicken breasts are especially good.

Steam two large chicken breast halves with bones 20 to 25 minutes. Let them cool slightly before removing the skin and bones and then gently shred the meat to measure 2 cups.

European cucumbers, available in most supermarkets, are the long, skinny ones that have fewer seeds.

Balsamic vinegar reduced to a syrup-like consistency makes a good substitute for higher-fat salad oil-based dressings. The balsamic has a light, sweet flavor and bit of tang that provides a nice contrast when tossed with greens and served with slightly tart oranges, melons and jicama.

Sprinkle a bit of chili powder over the fruit and serve with lime wedges for a quick, refreshing main-dish salad.

WINTER FRUIT SALAD

1 CUP BALSAMIC VINEGAR
2 TEASPOONS MINCED SHALLOTS
6 CUPS MIXED GREENS
SALT
FRESHLY CRACKED BLACK PEPPER
10 SLICES HONEYDEW MELON
10 SLICES JICAMA
12 ORANGE SEGMENTS
NEW MEXICO CHILI POWDER
LIME WEDGES

Combine vinegar and shallots in small saucepan over low heat and reduce to consistency of syrup, about 6 tablespoons, 4 to 5 minutes. Remove from heat and cool.

Toss greens with balsamic reduction to taste. Season with salt and pepper to taste.

Spoon greens onto serving plates. Arrange melon, jicama and orange pieces on top of greens. Sprinkle with chili powder to taste. Serve with lime wedges.

2 servings. Each serving: 215 calories; 182 mg sodium; 0 cholesterol; 1 gram fat; 48 grams carbohydrates; 4 grams protein; 2.71 grams fiber.

[Pizza, Pasta, Pane]

PIZZA POMODORO

2 teaspoons dry yeast
1/2 cup warm water (105 to 115 degrees)
1 teaspoon sugar
1/2 cup nonfat milk
2 teaspoons minced garlic
Salt
3 cups flour

2 tablespoons yellow cornmeal
1 1/2 tablespoons olive oil
4 to 5 thinly sliced Roma tomatoes
Pepper
2 tablespoons chopped fresh basil
1/3 cup shaved Parmesan cheese

Sprinkle yeast over warm water in large bowl. Stir until dissolved. Stir in sugar. Let stand until mixture begins to bubble. Stir in milk, garlic and 1 teaspoon salt.

Beat in 2 1/2 cups flour. Add enough of the remaining flour to make moderately stiff dough.

Turn dough out onto lightly floured surface and knead until smooth and satiny, 10 to 12 minutes. Shape into ball and place in lightly greased bowl, turning to grease all sides. Cover and let rise in warm place until doubled, about 45 minutes.

Punch dough down. Roll out on lightly floured surface to 13x9-inch rectangle. Place on lightly greased baking sheet sprinkled with cornmeal. Brush dough with half of oil. Cover with tomato slices slightly overlapping in rows. Brush tomatoes with remaining oil. Season tomatoes to taste with salt and pepper.

Bake at 350 degrees until edges of pizza dough are browned, 20 to 25 minutes. Sprinkle with fresh basil and cheese. Cut into 2x4 pieces.

8 servings. Each serving: 223 calories; 419 mg sodium; 3 mg cholesterol; 4 grams fat; 38 grams carbohydrates; 8 grams protein; 0.35 gram fiber.

Pizza doesn't have to be high in fat and calories to taste great. Instead of sausage and mozzerella, top your pizza with sliced fresh tomatoes, basil and Parmesan cheese. You'll not only be eating lighter, you'll be eating pizza that's closer to true Italian pizza as well.

Nonfat milk instead of olive oil is used in the dough for flavor and texture.

For the best flavor and to prevent singeing, be sure to sprinkle the fresh basil and Parmesan cheese over the pizza after it has been baked.

PIZZA, PASTA, PANE

Here, plum tomatoes and whole cloves of garlic are grilled on a heavy iron stove-top grill to produce a satisfying, slightly charred, flavor. They're combined with a good red wine for a sauce that not only has great flavor but is rich in color.

An extra bonus is the speediness of the recipe. In about 15 minutes, you'll have a flavorful low-fat pasta sauce that tastes as though it cooked much longer.

SPAGHETTI WITH CHARRED TOMATO SAUCE

2 POUNDS PLUM TOMATOES, HALVED LENGTHWISE
NONSTICK COOKING SPRAY
3 LARGE CLOVES GARLIC
1/2 CUP RED WINE
RED PEPPER FLAKES
1/2 TEASPOON SALT
1 TABLESPOON MINCED FRESH BASIL LEAVES
1 TABLESPOON MINCED FRESH OREGANO LEAVES
1/2 POUND SPAGHETTI OR LINGUINE, COOKED ACCORDING TO PACKAGE DIRECTIONS AND DRAINED
GRATED PARMESAN CHEESE

Grill tomatoes on pan grill sprayed with nonstick cooking spray until tomatoes are lightly charred on both sides and tender. Remove from grill and coarsely chop. Grill whole garlic cloves until charred and chop.

Combine chopped tomatoes and garlic in saucepan. Stir in red wine, red pepper flakes to taste and salt. Bring to boil. Reduce heat, cover and simmer until tomatoes cook into sauce, 15 to 20 minutes. Stir in basil and oregano. Serve over spaghetti. Sprinkle with Parmesan cheese to taste.

2 servings. Each serving: 561 calories; 639 mg sodium; 0 cholesterol; 3 grams fat; 109 grams carbohydrates; 18 grams protein; 3.33 grams fiber.

STUFFED CANNELLONI WITH PORCINI TOMATO SAUCE

6 CANNELLONI SHELLS

1/3 CUP DRIED PORCINI MUSHROOMS

1 SMALL ONION, MINCED

4 CLOVES GARLIC, MINCED

OLIVE OIL COOKING SPRAY

1 1/2 POUNDS TOMATOES, PEELED, SEEDED AND DICED

8 BASIL LEAVES, SHREDDED, PLUS 1 TABLESPOON CHOPPED

SALT

2 CUPS NONFAT RICOTTA CHEESE

1/3 CUP PLUS 2 TEASPOONS GRATED PARMESAN CHEESE

2 TABLESPOONS NONFAT EGG SUBSTITUTE

1/4 TEASPOON NUTMEG

1/8 TEASPOON CAYENNE PEPPER

1/4 POUND FRESH SPINACH, CHOPPED

Cook cannelloni shells in plenty of boiling salted water until tender, 12 to 15 minutes. Drain on paper towels and pat dry. Cover and set aside.

Put porcini mushrooms in small dish and barely cover with hot water. Allow to soak for 15 to 20 minutes. Squeeze throroughly before chopping. Reserve water for later addition to sauce.

Sauté onion and 2 minced cloves garlic in medium saucepan sprayed with olive oil cooking spray until tender, 2 to 3 minutes. Stir in tomatoes, shredded basil leaves and 1 teaspoon salt. Cook over low heat until mixture becomes hot and juices begin to come out of tomatoes. Stir in chopped porcini mushrooms and reserved soaking liquid. Reduce heat to simmer, cover and cook until sauce forms and tomatoes fall apart, about 15 minutes.

Combine ricotta cheese, 1/3 cup Parmesan cheese, remaining chopped basil, egg substitute, nutmeg, cayenne pepper and salt to taste. Sauté remaining 2 cloves garlic in skillet sprayed with nonstick cooking spray until tender, about 1 minute. Stir in spinach and sauté until wilted, 1 to 2 minutes. Squeeze excess juices out of spinach and stir into cheese mixture.

Pipe cheese filling into cannelloni shells. Arrange 3 filled shells in each of two oval baking dishes sprayed with cooking spray. Pour on tomato sauce and sprinkle 1 teaspoon grated Parmesan cheese over top of each. Bake at 350 degrees until hot and bubbly, 20 to 25 minutes.

2 servings. Each serving: 406 calories; 448 mg sodium; 15 mg cholesterol; 5 grams fat; 73 grams carbohydrates; 29 grams protein; 5.58 grams fiber.

PIZZA, PASTA, PANE

Cheesy looks can be deceiving. If the cheese is nonfat ricotta and low-fat Parmesan, you can have a rich dish like stuffed cannelloni without blowing your diet.

The sauce is made with fresh tomatoes that should be fully ripe for the best flavor. Dried mushrooms give a rich "meaty" flavor to the sauce. You can find them in the produce section of many supermarkets.

The recipe makes enough for two substantial servings but may easily be doubled or tripled.

And try piping the filling into the cooked shells; it's easier than trying to spoon it in.

Leafy Swiss chard combined with chicken broth makes a light sauce for pasta. I use the tamer green chard rather than its more colorful red sibling to get a milder flavor.

Allowing the egg substitute to set before completely stirring it into the broth gives the sauce a creamy look.

SWISS CHARD AND TOFU OVER CAPELLINI

2 OUNCES CAPELLINI OR ANGEL HAIR PASTA

SALT

WATER

3 CLOVES GARLIC, MINCED

1/3 CUP MINCED ONION

NONSTICK OLIVE OIL COOKING SPRAY

1 (14 1/2-OUNCE) CAN NONFAT LOW-SODIUM CHICKEN OR VEGETABLE BROTH

2 CUPS COARSELY CHOPPED SWISS CHARD

1 TABLESPOON CORNSTARCH

1/2 (12.3-OUNCE) CARTON LOW-FAT FIRM TOFU, WELL DRAINED AND CUBED

1/4 CUP NONFAT EGG SUBSTITUTE (EQUIVALENT TO 1 EGG)

Cook capellini in rapidly boiling salted water until just tender to the bite, about 2 minutes. Drain and keep warm until ready to serve.

Sauté garlic and onion in wok or heavy skillet sprayed with olive oil cooking spray until tender, 2 to 3 minutes. Stir in broth and Swiss chard. Bring to boil, then reduce heat and simmer over low heat until chard is tender, about 15 minutes.

Blend together 1 tablespoon water and cornstarch until smooth. Stir into simmering broth until blended. Heat and stir until thickened and clear, 1 to 2 minutes. Stir in tofu. Slowly drizzle in egg substitute and let stand until egg begins to set before stirring. Add salt to taste.

Serve over cooked capellini.

2 servings. Each serving: 221 calories; 509 mg sodium; 0 cholesterol; 2 grams fat; 32 grams carbohydrates; 19 grams protein; 0.61 gram fiber.

FRESH TOMATO LASAGNA

PIZZA, PASTA, PANE

HERBED TOMATO SAUCE
- 1 SMALL ONION, MINCED
- 1 LARGE CLOVE GARLIC, MINCED
- 1 TEASPOON OLIVE OIL
- 1 POUND RIPE TOMATOES
- 6 FRESH BASIL LEAVES, FINELY CHOPPED
- SALT, PEPPER

LASAGNA
- 1/2 CUP NONFAT RICOTTA CHEESE
- 2 TABLESPOONS NONFAT EGG SUBSTITUTE
- 1 TABLESPOON CHOPPED PARSLEY
- SALT, PEPPER
- 1/4 POUND SHIITAKE MUSHROOMS, SLICED
- 1/4 POUND BUTTON MUSHROOMS, SLICED
- SALT, PEPPER
- 3 TABLESPOONS SHREDDED BASIL
- HERBED TOMATO SAUCE
- 4 COOKED LASAGNA NOODLES, CUT IN HALF
- 1/4 CUP GRATED PARMESAN CHEESE

HERBED TOMATO SAUCE
Sauté onion and garlic in skillet with olive oil until tender. Stir in tomatoes and basil. Bring to simmer. Cook about 15 minutes, until thickened and sauce-like. Season to taste with salt and pepper.

LASAGNA
Combine ricotta cheese, nonfat egg substitute and parsley in bowl. Season to taste with salt and pepper. Set aside.

Cook shiitake and button mushrooms in heated nonstick skillet, shaking pan and stirring just until mushrooms are tender. Season to taste with salt and pepper. Stir in 1 tablespoon shredded basil.

Spoon 2 tablespoons Herbed Tomato Sauce into bottom of each of 2 individual 1 1/2-cup baking dishes. Spread sauce evenly to cover bottom of dish.

Arrange 2 pieces of lasagna noodles, cut to fit dish, on top of sauce in 1 baking dish. Repeat with second baking dish.

Spoon ricotta filling into baking dishes, then spoon over mushrooms.

Spread 2 tablespoons Herbed Tomato Sauce over mushrooms in each dish. Then sprinkle each with 1 tablespoon Parmesan cheese.

Top with remaining noodles, then spread remaining Herbed Tomato Sauce over noodles. Sprinkle top of each dish with 1 tablespoon Parmesan cheese. Bake at 375 degrees 20 to 30 minutes or until hot through and browned on top. Sprinkle 1 tablespoon shredded basil over top of each dish just before serving.

2 main-course servings or 4 side-dish servings. Each main-dish serving:
338 calories; 763 mg sodium; 14 mg cholesterol; 8 grams fat;
54 grams carbohydrates; 20 grams protein; 4.49 grams fiber.

Nonfat ricotta is the secret ingredient of this low-fat lasagna. With nonfat egg substitute, a little Parmesan cheese and some seasoning, it makes a rich-tasting filling.

You can sauté the mushrooms without oil by placing a nonstick skillet over high heat; once the pan is hot, add the mushrooms. The heat brings out the juices quickly and eliminates the need for butter or oil.

If you can't find flavorful tomatoes at the market, substitute canned, which are better than fresh when tomatoes are out of season.

PIZZA, PASTA, PANE

Ripe red tomatoes, a jar of roasted peppers and a can of nonfat chicken broth make a wonderfully flavored pasta sauce to spoon over rigatoni.

If you haven't used up all your fat grams for the day, combine freshly grated Parmesan cheese and dry Jack cheese in equal amounts and sprinkle a little over the top before serving.

RIGATONI WITH PORTABELLOS AND PEPPER SAUCE

NONSTICK COOKING SPRAY

3 CLOVES GARLIC, MINCED

1 CUP MINCED ONION

2 TOMATOES, CHOPPED

1 (15-OUNCE) JAR ROASTED RED PEPPERS, ROUGHLY CHOPPED

1 (14 1/2-OUNCE) CAN NONFAT CHICKEN BROTH

SALT

1 (1-POUND) PACKAGE BITE-SIZE RIGATONI

1 (6-OUNCE) PACKAGE PORTABELLO MUSHROOMS

1 BUNCH ARUGULA, TORN INTO BITE-SIZE PIECES

1/4 CUP CHOPPED BASIL

1 HUNGARIAN GREEN PEPPER, CUT INTO CROSSWISE SLICES

Spray large skillet with nonstick cooking spray. Add garlic and onion and sauté until tender, about 2 minutes. Stir in tomatoes and peppers. When hot, add chicken broth and bring to boil. Reduce heat and simmer to blend flavors, about 10 minutes. Purée in blender. Add salt to taste, about 1/2 teaspoon, and keep warm until ready to serve.

Cook rigatoni in boiling, salted water until just tender, 7 to 10 minutes. Drain and keep warm.

Spray stove-top grill pan with nonstick cooking spray and cook mushrooms on hot grill, spraying each side once to prevent sticking and turning to brown both sides until tender, 5 to 10 minutes, depending on size of mushrooms.

Let mushrooms cool slightly and slice. Toss with arugula and basil and stir into hot pasta until greens are slightly wilted.

Spoon pepper sauce over each serving and top with few Hungarian green pepper slices.

6 servings. Each serving: 341 calories; 117 mg sodium; 0 cholesterol; 1 gram fat; 69 grams carbohydrates; 14 grams protein; 1.27 grams fiber.

PAD THAI NOODLES

- 2 (10 1/2-ounce) packages firm, low-fat tofu
- Nonstick cooking spray
- Salt
- 1/3 cup fish sauce (*nuoc mam*)
- 1/3 cup sugar
- 2 teaspoons rice vinegar
- 2 teaspoons lime juice
- 1 tablespoon paprika
- Red pepper flakes
- 5 ounces Thai rice noodles
- 1/2 onion, cut into strips
- 3 cloves garlic, minced
- 1 cup shredded red cabbage
- 1 cup shredded nappa cabbage
- 3/4 cup shredded carrot
- 1/2 cup nonfat egg substitute
- 2 1/2 cups bean sprouts
- 2 tablespoons chopped peanuts
- Lime wedges

Drain tofu well, pat dry with paper towels and cut into 1-inch cubes.

Spray wok or heavy skillet with nonstick cooking spray and heat until hot. Add tofu cubes and fry, turning until browned on all sides, 5 to 7 minutes. Sprinkle lightly with salt to taste, remove from wok and set aside.

Combine fish sauce, sugar, vinegar, lime juice, paprika and red pepper flakes to taste in small bowl and set aside.

Add noodles to boiling water in large saucepan and cook 1 minute. Drain and rinse under cold water. Let stand in bowl of cold water until ready to use, then drain again.

Spray wok or heavy skillet with nonstick cooking spray and heat until sizzling hot. Add onion and stir-fry until golden brown, about 2 minutes. Add garlic and stir-fry 1 minute more.

Stir in red cabbage, nappa cabbage and 1/2 cup shredded carrot. Stir until vegetables are limp, 1 to 2 minutes. Add fish sauce mixture. Heat and stir until ingredients are mixed. Stir in tofu cubes and heat until hot through, about 1 minute. Stir in drained noodles.

Push ingredients to 1 side and add egg substitute. Let stand until egg sets, then stir to break up egg and mix into noodle mixture. Stir in 2 cups bean sprouts and heat until hot through, 1 to 2 minutes.

Spoon onto serving platter and sprinkle with chopped peanuts. Top with remaining 1/2 cup bean sprouts and 1/4 cup carrots. Serve with lime wedges.

3 servings. Each serving: 485 calories; 1,654 mg sodium; 0 cholesterol; 6 grams fat; 86 grams carbohydrates; 24 grams protein; 2.30 grams fiber.

PIZZA, PASTA, PANE

With a little egg substitute and a little low-fat tofu, you can have a lighter pad Thai.

Thai rice noodles, about the width of linguine, should be cooked about 1 minute, until they are limp but able to hold up in the stir-fry without falling apart. Letting them rest in a bowl of cold water after cooking prevents them from sticking together until it's time to add them to the stir-fry.

You want the bean sprouts to retain their crunch, so cook them briefly, just until warm.

PIZZA,
PASTA,
PANE

Kalamata olives and Parmesan cheese give this non-fat yogurt bread great flavor. Yogurt gives the bread tenderness, a fine texture and a full, slightly tangy flavor.

The olives and cheese contain some fat but can be eliminated.

OLIVE-YOGURT TURBAN

5 1/2 TO 6 1/2 CUPS FLOUR
2 PACKAGES ACTIVE DRY YEAST
1 CUP NONFAT MILK
2 TABLESPOONS SUGAR
2 TEASPOONS SALT
1 1/2 CUPS NONFAT PLAIN YOGURT

OLIVE OIL
1 CUP PITTED KALAMATA OLIVES, CHOPPED
2/3 CUP GRATED PARMESAN CHEESE
1/4 TEASPOON CRACKED BLACK PEPPER
CRUSHED ROCK SALT

Combine 2 cups flour and yeast in bowl. Heat milk, sugar and salt in saucepan. Heat to warm (115 to 120 degrees). Stir milk mixture into flour-yeast mixture until blended. Beat in yogurt until blended. Beat in enough remaining flour to make soft dough. Knead 10 minutes or until dough is smooth and elastic. Place in lightly oiled bowl, turning to coat outside of dough with oil. Cover and let rise until doubled, about 1 hour.

Punch dough down. Roll out on lightly floured surface to 36x8-inch rectangle.

Combine olives, cheese and pepper. Spoon down center of dough. Fold sides to center until they meet, pinching edges together. Roll up dough tightly from long end. Pinch edge of dough into roll to seal. Shape into turban on greased baking sheet. Cover and let rise until doubled. Lightly brush with olive oil. Sprinkle rock salt over bread to taste.

Bake at 425 degrees about 25 to 30 minutes or until browned and loaf sounds hollow when tapped. Remove to wire rack to cool until warm.

16 servings. Each serving: 201 calories; 590 mg sodium; 4 mg cholesterol; 3 grams fat; 35 grams carbohydrates; 8 grams protein; 0.20 grams fiber.

SKINNY BREAD STICKS

1 1/2 TEASPOONS DRY YEAST
1/2 CUP WARM WATER (105 TO 115 DEGREES)
1 1/2 TABLESPOONS OLIVE OIL
1 TEASPOON SALT
1 1/2 TO 2 CUPS FLOUR
2 EGG WHITES

Sprinkle yeast over warm water in mixing bowl and stir until dissolved. Let stand until foamy.

Stir in olive oil, salt and 1/2 cup flour.

Beat 1 egg white in separate bowl until stiff but not dry. Fold egg white into yeast-flour mixture. Beat in enough remaining flour to form soft dough. Knead dough about 5 minutes and place in oiled bowl. Cover with towel and let rise 15 minutes.

Knead dough. Roll dough out on lightly floured surface to 15x11-inch rectangle. Cut lengthwise into 1/2-inch strips. Twist strips of dough to form spiral patterns and place on lightly oiled baking sheets. Cover and let rise in warm room about 15 minutes.

Lightly beat remaining egg white and brush over bread sticks. (At this point you may, if you want, sprinkle the sticks with coarsely ground seasonings, such as black peppercorns, crushed Sichuan peppercorns, kosher salt, sesame seeds, poppy seeds, caraway seeds and crushed cumin seeds.) Bake at 350 degrees 20 to 25 minutes or until lightly browned. Remove to wire rack to cool.

22 bread sticks. Each bread stick, without optional flavorings: 41 calories; 219 mg sodium; trace cholesterol; 1 gram fat; 6 grams carbohydrates; 1 gram protein; 0.06 gram fiber.

PIZZA, PASTA, PANE

These bread sticks each have one gram of fat—not bad when you consider the fat you take in with a couple of potato chips.

Be creative when making them and sprinkle with different combinations of spices and herbs before baking. One of my favorite mixes is crushed Sichuan peppercorns and kosher salt.

PIZZA,
PASTA,
PANE

These substantial muffins, flavored with green chiles and corn, have only one gram of fat each. The traditional fat is replaced with cream-style corn; egg substitute is used instead of whole eggs and buttermilk takes the place of whole milk. Be careful not to over-mix or you will have tough muffins.

DOUBLE CORN MUFFINS

1 CUP YELLOW CORNMEAL
1 (8 3/4-OUNCE) CAN CREAM-STYLE CORN
1/4 CUP BUTTERMILK
1 1/2 CUPS FLOUR
1/3 CUP SUGAR
2 1/2 TEASPOONS BAKING POWDER
1 1/2 TEASPOONS BAKING SODA

1 TEASPOON SALT
1/4 CUP NONFAT EGG SUBSTITUTE (EQUIVALENT TO 1 EGG)
1/4 CUP LIGHT CORN SYRUP
1 (4-OUNCE) CAN DICED GREEN CHILES
1 (7-OUNCE) CAN MEXICORN, DRAINED

Mix cornmeal, cream-style corn and buttermilk in bowl. Let stand 20 minutes.

In separate bowl, stir together flour, sugar, baking powder, baking soda and salt. Stir in egg substitute, corn syrup, chiles, Mexicorn and reserved cornmeal mixture just until blended.

Grease 12 muffin cups or spray with nonstick cooking spray. Spoon muffin mixture into cups. Bake at 400 degrees until muffins are golden brown and cooked through, 15 to 20 minutes. Remove from pan to wire rack to cool slightly.

12 muffins. Each muffin: 170 calories; 424 mg sodium; 0 mg cholesterol; 1 gram fat; 3 8 grams carbohydrates; 4 grams protein; 0.73 gram fiber.

CALIFORNIA WRAP

- 1 CUP DICED, SEEDED PLUM TOMATOES
- 2 TEASPOONS MINCED BASIL
- 1 CLOVE GARLIC, MINCED
- 1/4 TEASPOON SALT
- 2 TEASPOONS OLIVE OIL
- 8 (9-INCH) LOW-FAT FLOUR TORTILLAS
- 1 CUP HUMMUS
- 1 CUCUMBER, THINLY SLICED
- 2 CUPS ALFALFA SPROUTS
- 1 CUP SHREDDED CARROTS
- 1/2 CUP CRUMBLED FARMER'S OR FETA CHEESE

Combine tomatoes, basil, garlic, salt and olive oil. Let stand about 15 minutes to blend flavors.

Heat each tortilla over gas flame or electric burner until warm and pliable.

For each wrap, spread 2 tablespoons hummus over tortilla to within 1/2 inch of edge. Top with single layer of cucumber slices, about 8 per tortilla. Sprinkle with 1/4 cup sprouts, 2 tablespoons carrots and 1 tablespoon cheese. Spoon about 2 tablespoons tomato-garlic mixture over all. Fold up bottom of tortilla, then fold one side over other, leaving top open.

8 wraps. Each wrap: 193 calories; 497 mg sodium; 10 mg cholesterol; 7 grams fat; 29 grams carbohydrates; 5 grams protein; 2.84 grams fiber.

HUMMUS

- 1 (15 1/2-OUNCE) CAN GARBANZO BEANS, DRAINED AND RINSED
- 1/4 CUP HOT WATER
- 2 TABLESPOONS SESAME TAHINEH
- 1 TEASPOON HUNGARIAN SWEET PAPRIKA
- 2 CLOVES GARLIC, CRUSHED
- 1/2 TEASPOON CUMIN
- 2 TABLESPOONS LEMON JUICE
- 1 TEASPOON SALT
- 1/4 TEASPOON CAYENNE PEPPER

Purée beans and water in blender or food processor until smooth. Blend in tahineh, paprika, garlic, cumin, lemon juice, salt and cayenne.

About 1 3/4 cup. Each 2-tablespoon serving: 66 calories; 173 mg sodium; 0 cholesterol; 2 grams fat; 10 grams carbohydrates; 3 grams protein; 0.95 gram fiber.

PIZZA, PASTA, PANE

Wraps are a little like baked potatoes: It's not the wrap but what you put in it that makes the difference. This wrap is spread with homemade hummus, rather than mayonnaise. Lots of fresh vegetables—almost any will do—go inside. The diced tomatoes flavored with garlic and herbs act as a low-fat dressing that gives the rest of the vegetables flavor. Serve with a dollop of nonfat yogurt for extra creaminess.

Tahineh, used in the hummus, is a sesame paste that can be found at health food and specialty stores.

PIZZA, PASTA, PANE

This is a sandwich for people who love egg salad but feel a twinge of guilt every time they eat one. First, there's no egg in the egg salad. Light tofu is drained, then mashed and combined with celery, onion, seasonings and nonfat mayonnaise. Turmeric and everyday yellow mustard give the mix its characteristic egg salad yellow color. The flavor comes out best when chilled.

Buy a good-tasting low-fat, whole-grain bread to make the sandwich great.

SUMMARY "EGG" SALAD AND FRESH VEGETABLE SANDWICHES

"EGG" SALAD

1 (10 1/2-ounce) box extra-firm light tofu
1/4 cup nonfat mayonnaise
1/3 cup minced celery
1 teaspoon prepared mustard
1 teaspoon cider vinegar
1/2 teaspoon lemon juice
1 teaspoon minced dill
2 tablespoons minced green onion tops
1 teaspoon ground turmeric
3/4 teaspoon salt or to taste
Freshly ground black pepper

ASSEMBLY

12 slices low-fat whole-grain bread
Nonfat mayonnaise
3 cups shredded carrots
1 (4-ounce) carton alfalfa sprouts
Romaine leaves

"EGG" SALAD

Drain tofu well. Mash with fork. Stir in mayonnaise, celery, mustard, vinegar, lemon juice, dill, onion, turmeric, sea salt and pepper to taste. Chill about 2 hours.

ASSEMBLY

Lightly spread bread slices with nonfat mayonnaise. Layer about 1/2 cup shredded carrots on 6 slices bread. Top each with alfalfa sprouts, then spoon about 1/4 cup "egg" salad on top of each sandwich and spread to edges. Top each with several romaine leaves, then cover each sandwich with remaining bread slices. Cut into quarters and serve.

1 1/2 cups egg salad for 6 sandwiches. Each sandwich: 225 calories; 737 mg sodium; 0 cholesterol; 3 grams fat; 37 grams carbohydrates; 12 grams protein; 4.67 grams fiber.

Each 1/4-cup serving egg salad alone: 29 calories; 368 mg sodium; 0 cholesterol; 1 gram fat; 2 grams carbohydrates; 3 grams protein; 0.11 gram fiber.

BERRY BLAST, PAGE 20

OVEN-FRIED ZUCCHINI, PAGE 21

CAVIAR-STUFFED POTATOES, PAGE 24

ESCAROLE CHICKEN SOUP, PAGE 33

BAJA SQUID SALAD, PAGE 41

SHRIMP AND GARLIC COLESLAW, PAGE 41

SHREDDED CHICKEN SALAD, PAGE 51

WINTER FRUIT SALAD, PAGE 52

PAD THAI NOODLES, PAGE 59

STEAMED SALMON WITH TARAGON SAUCE, PAGE 68

CHINESE ROCK COD WITH VEGETABLES, PAGE 69

DILLED TURKEY MEAT BALLS, PAGE 79

TURKEY FAJITAS, PAGE 80

SAVORY BAKED SWEET POTATOES, PAGE 89

EGGPLANT STACK, PAGE 91

HONEYDEW ICE, PAGE 99

Meat, Fish and Poultry

MIXED VEGETABLE AND BEEF STIR-FRY

1 SMALL ONION, SLICED THIN
1 TABLESPOON MINCED GARLIC
NONSTICK COOKING SPRAY
1/2 POUND LEAN TOP SIRLOIN, CUT INTO STRIPS
1 TABLESPOON MINCED GINGER ROOT
3 CUPS BROCCOLI FLORETS, BLANCHED AND DRAINED
2 CUPS SLICED MUSHROOMS
1 TEASPOON CORNSTARCH
1/4 CUP NONFAT CHICKEN BROTH
1/4 CUP SOY SAUCE
1 (5 1/2-OUNCE) CAN BABY CORN, DRAINED
PEPPER

Stir-fry onions and garlic in hot skillet or wok sprayed with nonstick cooking spray over high heat until onions are translucent, 2 to 3 minutes. Remove to large bowl.

Spray wok with cooking spray if needed and add beef and ginger. Stir-fry until beef is browned. Remove and add to onions and garlic.

Spray wok with nonstick cooking spray if needed and add broccoli and mushrooms. Stir-fry vegetables until tender-crisp. Add to mixture in bowl.

Combine cornstarch and chicken broth. Add to pan along with soy sauce. Cook, stirring until thickened. Add ingredients in bowl and toss with sauce. Stir in baby corn. Heat through. Season to taste with pepper. Serve with steamed rice.

4 servings. Each serving: 156 calories; 1,094 mg sodium; 26 mg cholesterol; 3 grams fat; 21 grams carbohydrates; 16 grams protein; 1.52 grams fiber.

Stir-fry dishes are lower in fat than the average main course because less oil is used. But some cooks get complacent when making stir-fries and start padding the mix with high-fat foods. To keep the fat low, remember to use only enough meat in stir-fries to flavor the dish. Use vegetables for bulk.

This recipe uses lean top sirloin, but to keep this a true low-fat dish, be sure to trim the meat of all visible fat before cutting it into strips.

Flank steak is one of the skinnier cuts of beef. And when trimmed of any surface fat and cooked properly, it can be one of the tastiest and most economical steaks on the market.

A spiced seasoning rub and garlic are used not only to tenderize this normally tough cut but to give it great flavor. The dish tastes—and looks—best when there are one or two pieces of garlic in each slice.

Though the meat should marinate in the refrigerator one or two days, the steak can be grilled and served within minutes.

GRILLED FLANK STEAK ADOBO

ADOBO SEASONING RUB
- 2 TEASPOONS PASILLA CHILE POWDER
- 2 TEASPOONS PAPRIKA
- 1 3/4 TEASPOONS OREGANO
- 1 TEASPOON GROUND CUMIN
- 1 TEASPOON DRY MUSTARD
- 2 TEASPOONS SALT
- 1/4 TEASPOON CAYENNE PEPPER

STEAK
- 1 (1 1/2-POUND) FLANK STEAK
- 3 TO 4 CLOVES GARLIC, CUT INTO SLIVERS

ADOBO SEASONING RUB

Combine chile powder, paprika, oregano, cumin, mustard, salt and cayenne in bowl. Store in covered container.

STEAK

Trim excess fat from flank steak. Lightly score surface of both sides of meat in crisscross diamond pattern. Over top surface of meat, with knife, make slits large enough to insert 1 to 2 slivers of garlic. Place garlic into slits. Rub Adobo Seasoning Rub over both sides of meat to cover. Cover and refrigerate 1 to 2 days.

Spray grill pan or grill with nonstick cooking spray, add meat and grill over high heat until steak is rare inside and outside is charred, 7 to 9 minutes. Slice meat thinly on diagonal across grain.

6 servings. Each serving: 142 calories; 858 mg sodium; 43 mg cholesterol; 7 grams fat; 2 grams carbohydrates; 18 grams protein; 0.46 grams fiber.

SHRIMP FRIED RICE

SESAME OIL-FLAVORED NONSTICK COOKING SPRAY

6 GREEN ONIONS

1 POUND MEDIUM SHRIMP, PEELED AND DEVEINED

4 CLOVES GARLIC, MINCED

1 SMALL CARROT, CUT INTO JULIENNE STRIPS

4 CUPS COLD COOKED WHITE RICE

1 TABLESPOON SOY SAUCE

1 CUP NONFAT EGG SUBSTITUTE (EQUIVALENT TO 4 EGGS)

2 CUPS SHREDDED SPINACH

1 CUP FROZEN PEAS

1 CUP FRESH GREEN BEANS, CUT INTO 2-INCH PIECES, BLANCHED AND DRAINED

SALT

RED PEPPER FLAKES

Spray grill pan with cooking spray and heat. Grill 5 onions until brown and tender. Remove from grill and cut into 1-inch pieces. Set aside.

Grill shrimp until opaque on both sides and cooked through, 3 to 4 minutes. Set aside.

Spray wok with cooking spray. Stir-fry garlic and carrot 1 to 2 minutes. Add rice and continue to stir-fry 4 to 5 minutes until hot. Stir in soy sauce.

Make well in center and add 1/2 cup of egg substitute. Cook until bottom is set. Stir to break up eggs. Then stir into rice.

Stir in grilled shrimp, onions, spinach, peas and beans. Season to taste with salt and red pepper flakes.

Spray 6-inch omelet pan with nonstick cooking spray. Pour in remaining egg substitute and cook until eggs are set. Remove from skillet and cut into julienne strips. Lightly stir into rice. Cut remaining green onion into diagonal slices and garnish rice.

4 servings. Each serving: 469 calories; 649 mg sodium; 172 mg cholesterol; 3 grams fat; 71 grams carbohydrates; 38 grams protein; 1.64 grams fiber.

MEAT, FISH AND POULTRY

Fried rice can be quite low in fat, especially if you use egg substitute and shrimp instead of pork meat and whole eggs for flavoring.

Remember that cooked rice should be cold for stir-frying so it doesn't turn gummy.

MEAT, FISH AND POULTRY

The aromatic scent of tarragon and pink, green and black peppercorns is what makes this simple salmon spectacular. Serve the salmon chilled with a toss of watercress and arugula or hot right out of the steamer. If you choose to serve it hot, steam a few fresh beans or squash with the fish.

STEAMED SALMON WITH TARRAGON SAUCE

1/3 CUP NONFAT SOUR CREAM
1/3 CUP LOW-FAT MAYONNAISE
1/2 TEASPOON DIJON MUSTARD
1 TEASPOON GRATED ONION
2 TEASPOONS MINCED TARRAGON
1 TEASPOON LEMON JUICE
TRI-COLORED PEPPERCORNS, CRUSHED
SEA SALT
1 (1-POUND) SALMON STEAK
TARRAGON LEAVES
1 LEMON, SLICED
1 BUNCH WATERCRESS

Combine sour cream, mayonnaise, mustard, onion, tarragon, lemon juice and 1/4 teaspoon crushed peppercorns. Stir in salt to taste. Cover and chill.

Season salmon steak to taste with salt and crushed peppercorns. Line rack of steamer pan with tarragon leaves. Place fish on rack and tuck lemon slices around fish. Steam, covered, about 10 minutes. Remove to platter and let cool. Cover and chill.

Serve fish on bed of watercress. Serve tarragon sauce on side.

4 servings. Each serving with 1 tablespoon sauce: 172 calories; 188 mg sodium; 50 mg cholesterol; 8.5 grams fat; 3 grams carbohydrates; 19.5 grams protein; 0.07 gram fiber.

CHINESE ROCK COD WITH VEGETABLES

1 SMALL CARROT, SLICED
1 POUND ROCK COD STEAK
NONSTICK COOKING SPRAY
2 (1/4-INCH) SLICES PLUS 2 TEASPOONS SLIVERED GINGER ROOT
2 TEASPOONS SLIVERED GARLIC
1 GREEN ONION, CUT INTO 1-INCH PIECES
1 (5.95-OUNCE) CAN STRAW MUSHROOMS
1 CUP NONFAT CHICKEN BROTH
4 TEASPOONS CORNSTARCH
2 TEASPOONS SOY SAUCE
1/2 TEASPOON SALT
2 TEASPOONS SESAME OIL
4 TEASPOONS OYSTER SAUCE

Cook sliced carrot in boiling water until tender, about 5 minutes. Drain and set aside.

Remove skin and bones from fish. Cut fish into 2-inch pieces.

Spray wok with nonstick cooking spray; heat until hot. Add 2 slices ginger. When ginger begins to brown, push to 1 side and add fish. Lower heat and stir-fry fish about 3 minutes until it begins to brown and is almost done. Remove fish from wok and set aside. Discard ginger slices.

Spray wok with cooking spray and heat until sizzling. Quickly sauté garlic, 2 teaspoons slivered ginger root and onion until tender, about 1 minute. Add mushrooms and reserved carrots. Stir-fry until hot.

Add enough chicken broth to cornstarch to blend until smooth, then stir in remaining broth, soy sauce, salt, sesame oil and oyster sauce. Stir into vegetables. Bring to boil. Stir and simmer just until thickened and clear.

Stir in fish. Heat just until hot through and fish flakes when tested with a fork, about 1 minute.

4 servings. Each serving: 144 calories; 1,010 mg sodium; 34 mg cholesterol; 3 grams fat; 10 grams carbohydrates; 18 grams protein; 0.56 grams fiber.

MEAT, FISH AND POULTRY

Stir-fries can be deceptively high in fat. Because we see all the wholesome vegetables that go into them, we tend not to think about how much oil might be involved. But it can be plenty. In the case of fish, stir-frying can be almost like deep frying.

The good news is that you can sauté the fish in a wok sprayed with nonstick cooking spray with wonderful results. You just have to make sure that the wok is hot and that the bottom is well covered with the spray.

MEAT, FISH AND POULTRY

Swordfish is firm and meaty-tasting, an ideal fish for grilling. For even more flavor, rub it with garlic and spices. After seasoning, flatten it into a paillard for quicker cooking.

It's a good idea to have the salad greens arranged on chilled serving plates before putting the fish on the grill. You want to serve the fish as soon as it's off the grill.

This is excellent with a little lime juice squeezed over it. Serve hot sauce on the side.

PAILLARD OF SWORDFISH

1/2 POUND SWORDFISH, ABOUT 1/2-INCH THICK
1/2 TEASPOON CUMIN SEEDS
1/2 TEASPOON MEXICAN OREGANO
1 TEASPOON PAPRIKA
1 CLOVE GARLIC, CRUSHED
SALT
3 CUPS MIXED GREENS
1/4 CUP SHREDDED FETA OR COTIJA CHEESE
1 TOMATO, CHOPPED
NONSTICK COOKING SPRAY
JUICE OF 1 LIME
LIME SLICES

Cut fish into 2 pieces. Coarsely grind cumin seeds and oregano together in mortar with pestle. Stir in paprika.

Rub crushed garlic over both sides of each piece of fish, then rub spice mixture all over fish. Sprinkle with salt.

Put each piece of fish between 2 pieces of wax paper and gently pound with wooden mallet until fish is about 1/8 inch thick.

Divide mixed greens onto 2 chilled serving plates. Sprinkle shredded cheese and chopped tomato over greens on each plate.

Spray stove-top grill or outdoor grill lightly with nonstick cooking spray. Remove wax paper from fish paillards and place on grill. Cook on hot grill just until fish tests done and is browned on both sides, 1 to 2 minutes per side. Sprinkle fish with lime juice. Remove fish to salad plates.

Garnish with lime slices and serve.

2 servings. Each serving: 177 calories; 361 mg sodium; 45 mg cholesterol; 7 grams fat; 9 grams carbohydrates; 22 grams protein; 1.29 grams fiber.

SHRIMP TOSTADA WITH SPICY CILANTRO VINAIGRETTE

1/2 TEASPOON MEXICAN OREGANO

1 SMALL SERRANO CHILE

2 TABLESPOONS CHOPPED CILANTRO

1/4 CUP MINCED RED ONION

1 SMALL (YELLOW) GUERO CHILE

1/4 CUP LIME JUICE

1 POUND PEELED ROCK SHRIMP, COOKED

1 (15-OUNCE) CAN BLACK BEANS

1 ONION, CUT INTO 1/2-INCH SLICES

2 CLOVES GARLIC

MESQUITE-FLAVORED NONSTICK COOKING SPRAY

4 CORN TORTILLAS

2 CUPS SHREDDED ROMAINE LETTUCE

1 SMALL RED TOMATO, CUT IN WEDGES

1 SMALL YELLOW TOMATO, CUT IN WEDGES

Toast oregano in small ungreased skillet over low heat until fragrant, about 1 minute. Slice 1/2 serrano chile and reserve for garnish. Mince remaining 1/2 and combine with cilantro, red onion, guero chile, lime juice and toasted oregano. Stir in cooked shrimp. Cover and chill several hours or overnight.

Drain beans, reserving liquid. Set aside.

Cook onion slices and garlic on grill sprayed with mesquite-flavored nonstick cooking spray until charred on all sides and tender. Chop onion and garlic.

Cook beans over low heat in skillet sprayed with nonstick cooking spray, mashing over low heat until puréed. Stir in chopped onion and garlic. Stir in about 1/3 cup reserved liquid from beans and simmer several minutes, stirring occasionally.

Lightly spray both sides of tortillas with nonstick cooking spray and place in single layer on baking sheet. Bake at 425 degrees 8 to 10 minutes until lightly browned and crisp. Remove from oven and let cool.

For each tostada, spread about 2 tablespoons bean mixture over tortilla. Top with 1/2 cup shredded romaine. Spoon 1/4 of shrimp over top. Garnish with few red and yellow tomato wedges and reserved slices serrano chile.

4 tostadas. Each tostada: 318 calories; 170 mg sodium; 110 mg cholesterol; 3 grams fat; 46 grams carbohydrates; 28 grams protein; 3.98 grams fiber.

MEAT, FISH AND POULTRY

Tortillas are typically fried in lots of oil to make them crisp. For this low-fat version, they are sprayed with nonstick cooking spray, then baked in the oven until crisp. Use corn tortillas because they're lower in fat than flour tortillas and crisp up better in the oven.

The refried black beans are a short-cut version using canned beans. To give them a taste reminiscent of smoky bacon, use mesquite cooking spray.

To toast oregano for the shrimp marinade, heat it in a small skillet until the aroma comes out and it begins to lightly brown.

MEAT, FISH AND POULTRY

A traditional twice-baked potato is normally filled with butter, cream, cheese and sometimes sour cream—a high-fat spud. A true brandade, most often served as a spread for French bread, is usually a purée made with salt cod, olive oil and milk and sometimes garlic and potato.

This recipe combines both ideas to produce a new low-fat way to serve potatoes: twice-baked potatoes brandade. Each serving has 5 grams of fat. A traditional twice-baked potato can contain 22 grams of fat.

TWICE-BAKED POTATOES BRANDADE

1 POUND BONED SALT CODFISH
4 LARGE BOILING POTATOES, ABOUT 10 OUNCES EACH
6 CLOVES GARLIC, MINCED
NONSTICK COOKING SPRAY
1 TO 1 1/4 CUPS NONFAT CHICKEN BROTH
SALT
CRACKED BLACK PEPPER
2 TEASPOONS BUTTER, MELTED
PAPRIKA
1 TABLESPOON NONFAT EGG SUBSTITUTE

Put salt cod in large glass bowl, add water to cover, then cover and refrigerate 1 to 2 days, depending on saltiness of cod. Drain and replace water twice.

Drain, then cover salt cod with fresh water in large saucepan. Bring to boil. Remove from heat, let stand 10 minutes, drain, then flake fish.

Bake potatoes at 425 degrees until fork tender, about 1 hour. Cut top 1/4 off each potato. Scoop hot potato insides out of shells and into potato ricer. Press potatoes through ricer into large bowl. Reserve potato shells.

Lightly sauté garlic in skillet sprayed with cooking spray. Add garlic to potatoes. Stir in flaked fish. Add enough chicken broth to get mashed potato consistency, then season with salt and pepper to taste. Process mixture in food processor until light and fluffy. Be careful not to overmix; potatoes can become gummy. Fill pastry bag with mixture and pipe into hollowed-out shells. Brush tops with butter. Sprinkle with paprika to taste. Brush tops with egg substitute. Bake at 400 degrees until potatoes are hot through and golden brown on top, 30 to 45 minutes.

4 servings. Each serving: 517 calories; 6,637 mg sodium; 143 mg cholesterol; 5 grams fat; 53 grams carbohydrates; 64 grams protein; 1.29 gram fiber.

SCALLOPS IN CREAM SAUCE OVER PAN-FRIED NOODLES

3 CLOVES GARLIC, MINCED

1 POUND SCALLOPS

1 TEASPOON BUTTER

1 (14 1/2-OUNCE) CAN NONFAT CHICKEN BROTH

2 CUPS NONFAT MILK

2 TABLESPOONS DRY WHITE WINE

2 TABLESPOONS NONFAT DRY MILK

1/2 CUP FLOUR

1/4 CUP NONFAT EGG SUBSTITUTE (EQUIVALENT TO 1 EGG)

MESQUITE-FLAVORED NONSTICK COOKING SPRAY

1/2 POUND PERCIATELLI NOODLES

1 (3-OUNCE) PACKAGE SEASONED SMELT ROE

SALT, PEPPER

Rub 2 cloves minced garlic over scallops in glass baking dish. Cover. Let stand while preparing cream sauce and noodles.

Sauté 1 clove garlic in butter in large saucepan. Set aside 3/4 cup chicken broth. Add remaining broth to saucepan. Stir in milk, wine and nonfat dry milk. Heat to boiling, stirring constantly. Blend together remaining chicken broth and flour until smooth. Stir into boiling sauce.

Heat and stir until thickened, 1 to 2 minutes. Blend little of hot sauce into egg substitute to temper egg. Return all to saucepan. Heat and stir until slightly thickened. Set sauce aside and keep warm while pan frying noodles and grilling scallops.

Grill scallops on hot pan grill sprayed with cooking spray until scallops are just cooked through and tender, 2 to 3 minutes.

Cook noodles according to package directions. Drain well. Divide noodles into 4 portions shaping into round nest to fit bottom of wok. Slide noodles, 1 portion at time, into hot wok sprayed with cooking spray. Let noodles brown on bottom, then turn to brown other side.

Spoon scallops over noodles on plates. Stir 1/4 cup roe into cream sauce. Season to taste with salt and pepper. Spoon over scallops and noodles. Garnish with remaining smelt roe.

4 servings. Each serving: 272 calories; 861 mg sodium; 158 mg cholesterol; 7 grams fat; 23 grams carbohydrates; 30 grams protein; 0.08 gram fiber.

MEAT, FISH AND POULTRY

Scallops in buerre blanc is a nouvelle cuisine classic. Here, it's served over crisp, pan-fried noodles and made lower in fat by reducing the butter to 1 teaspoon and substituting nonfat milk and dry milk for the usual cream.

To get the smoky flavor of restaurant-style fried noodles, spray the wok with mesquite-flavored nonstick cooking spray.

MEAT, FISH AND POULTRY

Everyone knows that mayonnaise is what gives tuna salad most of its fat. Not everyone knows what to do about it. Yogurt, thickened overnight by draining in a colander, is a good substitute for mayonnaise and tastes terrific.

Spread the tuna salad on a tortilla-like lavash, roll it, then slice it into rounds and you'll have lunch for six. Serve the sandwiches with soup or salad. Or double the recipe and put the rolls out on a platter during a party; they're easy to eat standing up.

For extra crunch, a layer of romaine or leaf lettuce may be rolled into the sandwich.

LAVASH ROLLED WITH SMOKED TUNA SALAD AND FRESH VEGETABLES

2 CUPS PLAIN YOGURT

1 (9-OUNCE) CAN TUNA, PACKED IN WATER, DRAINED AND FLAKED

1/2 CUP MINCED CELERY

1 TABLESPOON GRATED ONION

1 TABLESPOON PREPARED HORSERADISH

2 TEASPOONS LEMON JUICE

1/4 TEASPOON LIQUID SMOKE, OPTIONAL

1 TEASPOON SALT

1 LAVASH

1/2 (6-OUNCE) CARTON ALFALFA SPROUTS

3 ROMA TOMATOES, CHOPPED

1 SMALL RED ONION, SLICED PAPER-THIN

Use yogurt strainer or line colander or kitchen strainer with double thickness of damp cheesecloth and set in bowl, keeping bottom of strainer several inches above bottom of bowl. Spoon in yogurt. Cover and chill 5 to 24 hours.

Combine drained yogurt, tuna, celery, onion, horseradish, lemon juice, liquid smoke and salt. Cover and chill.

To assemble, spread tuna mixture over surface of 1 lavash to within 1 inch of edges. Sprinkle alfalfa sprouts, tomatoes and sliced red onion over tuna. Roll up lavash from long edge. Cut roll into 1 1/2-inch slices to serve. Lavash may be rolled and chilled 1 hour before serving.

6 servings. Each serving: 330 calories; 784 mg sodium; 17 mg cholesterol; 5 grams fat; 50 grams carbohydrates; 25 grams protein; 3.56 grams fiber.

LOW-FAT '50S TUNA NOODLE CASSEROLE

MEAT, FISH AND POULTRY

1/4 CUP MINCED ONION

1 CUP SLICED CELERY

2 TEASPOONS BUTTER

1/4 POUND MUSHROOMS, FINELY CHOPPED

1/4 CUP FLOUR

2 CUPS NONFAT MILK

2 TABLESPOONS NONFAT DRY MILK

1 CUP FROZEN PEAS

SALT

WHITE PEPPER

1/4 POUND MEDIUM NOODLES COOKED ACCORDING TO PACKAGE DIRECTIONS AND DRAINED

BUTTER-FLAVORED NONSTICK COOKING SPRAY

1 (12-1/2 OUNCE) CAN TUNA PACKED IN WATER, DRAINED

2 CUPS FAT-FREE POTATO CHIPS, COARSELY CRUSHED

Sauté onion and celery in butter until tender. Add mushrooms and sauté few minutes, until liquid comes out of mushrooms. Stir in flour. Gradually blend in milk then nonfat dry milk. Heat, stirring constantly, to boiling. Boil and stir until thickened, about 1 minute. Stir in peas. Season to taste with salt and white pepper.

Spoon 1/3 of drained noodles evenly onto 9-inch baking dish sprayed with cooking spray. Arrange 1/2 drained tuna over noodles. Pour 1/3 sauce over tuna, spreading to edges. Repeat layers. Top with remaining noodles and sauce. Sprinkle crushed potato chips evenly over top of baking dish. Bake at 375 degrees 25 to 30 minutes or until top is lightly browned and casserole is hot through.

6 servings. Each serving: 287 calories; 439 mg sodium; 34 mg cholesterol; 3 grams fat; 36 grams carbohydrates; 27 grams protein; 1.60 gram fiber.

Remember the tuna noodle casserole? The one with the crushed potato chips on the top? This version has only three grams of fat compared to 21 grams in the original recipe. And there are fewer than half the calories. Just using fat-free potato chips saved 3 grams of fat per serving. And by using water-pack tuna instead of oil-pack, you can use a larger can of tuna for more flavor.

MEAT, FISH AND POULTRY

Sake kasu or sake lees is the sediment left when sake is fermented. It is sold in plastic bags in the refrigerated section of Japanese markets. When combined with mirin, a sweet rice wine also found in Japanese markets, sake, brown sugar and salt, it makes a thin, creamy marinade for fish.

After grilling, the fish will be lightly glazed and have a slightly sweet flavor.

Serve with asparagus spears or Chinese broccoli.

RED SNAPPER MARINATED IN SAKE LEES

3/4 CUP SAKE LEES
3/4 CUP MIRIN
1 TABLESPOON DRY SAKE
3 TABLESPOONS BROWN SUGAR
1 TEASPOON SALT
4 (6-OUNCE) RED SNAPPER FILLETS
NONSTICK COOKING SPRAY OR OLIVE OIL

Process sake lees and mirin in blender or food processor until smooth and creamy. Add sake, brown sugar and salt and blend.

Pour half of marinade into glass baking dish. Put fish filets in single layer over marinade in dish and top with remaining marinade, spreading to cover filets. Cover with plastic wrap and marinate in refrigerator overnight.

When ready to cook, remove fish from dish and scrape off excess marinade. Lightly mist fish with nonstick cooking spray or olive oil. Spray stove-top grill pan or broiler pan with nonstick cooking spray. Grill on stove-top or broil until filets flake easily with fork and are brown on both sides, about 3 to 6 minutes per side depending on thickness of filets.

4 servings. Each serving: 293 calories; 814 mg sodium; 50 mg cholesterol; 2 grams fat; 30 grams carbohydrates; 40 grams protein; 0 fiber.

SEAFOOD IN BLACK BEAN SAUCE

1 POUND MANILA CLAMS
4 STONE CRAB CLAWS
4 JUMBO SEA SCALLOPS
1 TABLESPOON PEANUT OIL
2 TABLESPOONS CHOPPED GARLIC
1 1/2 TABLESPOONS CHOPPED GINGER ROOT
2 TABLESPOONS CHOPPED GREEN ONIONS
3 TABLESPOONS FERMENTED BLACK BEANS
3 TABLESPOONS LIGHT SOY SAUCE
2 TABLESPOONS RICE WINE
2 TEASPOONS SUGAR
1/2 CUP NONFAT LOW-SODIUM CHICKEN BROTH
1 TEASPOON SESAME OIL
4 SLICES LEMON
8 LARGE SHRIMP WITH HEADS
CILANTRO LEAVES

Divide clams, crab claws and scallops between 2 deep-dish serving plates or pie plates that will fit in steamer basket.

Heat peanut oil in wok until hot. Add garlic, ginger and onions and stir-fry until tender, about 1 minute. Stir in black beans and stir-fry 1 minute. Stir in soy sauce, wine, sugar and broth. Bring to simmer and stir in sesame oil. Pour evenly over seafood on each plate and tuck lemon slices into seafood.

Cover each plate with foil. Steam 1 plate 5 minutes. Add 4 shrimp and steam until clams open, shrimp are pink and scallops are no longer translucent, about 5 minutes. Remove from steamer and cover with foil to keep warm. Repeat with second plate of seafood and remaining 4 shrimp. Sprinkle with cilantro leaves.

2 servings. Each serving: 449 calories; 1,248 mg sodium; 162 mg cholesterol; 13 grams fat; 17 grams carbohydrates; 54 grams protein; 0.21 gram fiber.

MEAT, FISH AND POULTRY

Steaming brings out subtle nuances in food that often are lost with other cooking methods. It is an easy, gentle way of cooking food without the addition of fat. It also has the benefit of retaining most of the natural juices and nutrients in foods so that little or none is lost in the cooking process.

MEAT, FISH AND POULTRY

When the weather is hot, I like to bake this terrine in the morning while it's still cool, then keep it on hand in the refrigerator for a quick light dinner.

Check the labels on the ground turkey package for the fat percentages; they often vary.

Slice the terrine thin and serve it on French bread with crunchy lettuce, thin sliced red onions and tomatoes and a touch of mustard. Accompany this dish with a platter of radishes and cornichons.

CHILLED FLORENTINE TURKEY TERRINE

1 POUND MUSHROOMS
2 CLOVES GARLIC, MINCED
1 TABLESPOON BUTTER
1 (10-OUNCE) PACKAGE FROZEN CHOPPED SPINACH, THAWED AND WELL-DRAINED
2 TABLESPOONS MINCED SAGE
2 POUNDS GROUND TURKEY BREAST
1 CUP CHOPPED ONION
1/2 CUP NONFAT EGG SUBSTITUTE (EQUIVALENT TO 2 EGGS)
1 1/2 TEASPOONS SALT
1/2 TEASPOON BLACK PEPPER
BUTTER-FLAVORED NONSTICK COOKING SPRAY

Clean mushrooms and and coarsely chop.

Sauté mushrooms and garlic in skillet over medium-high with butter until tender and water has evaporated. Stir in spinach and sage until mixed. Remove from heat and set aside.

Combine turkey, onion, egg substitute, salt, pepper and hot spinach mixture in large bowl. Lightly mix until ingredients are blended. Pat into 1 (9x5-inch) loaf dish sprayed with butter-flavored nonstick cooking spray. Loaf will be full to top. Pat sides beneath top edges of dish and mound in center.

Cover with foil and bake 30 minutes at 350 degrees. Remove foil and continue to bake 1 hour. For best flavor, let cool to warm, then chill. Slice thin and serve with desired garnishes.

8 servings. Each serving: 146 calories; 548 mg sodium; 57 mg cholesterol; 2 grams fat; 7 grams carbohydrates; 25 grams protein; 0.97 gram fiber.

DILLED TURKEY MEAT BALLS

1 POUND GROUND TURKEY BREAST
2 TABLESPOONS MINCED ONION
2 CLOVES GARLIC, MINCED
1/2 CUP NONFAT EGG SUBSTITUTE (EQUIVALENT TO 2 EGGS)
1/4 CUP MINCED FRESH DILL WEED
1 TEASPOON SALT
1/4 TEASPOON BLACK PEPPER
BUTTER-FLAVORED NONSTICK COOKING SPRAY
2 TEASPOONS BUTTER
1 CUP CHOPPED MUSHROOMS
1 TABLESPOON FLOUR
1 CUP NONFAT CHICKEN BROTH
1 CUP NONFAT MILK
2 TABLESPOONS LEMON JUICE
DASH WHITE PEPPER

Combine ground turkey, onion, garlic, 1/4 cup egg substitute, 2 tablespoons dill weed, salt and pepper. Lightly mix just until ingredients are blended. Shape into 16 balls.

Spray 10-inch skillet with butter-flavored nonstick cooking spray. Add butter to skillet and heat until melted. Add meat balls to skillet and brown on all sides.

Remove meat balls from skillet. Add mushrooms to skillet and sauté just until mushrooms are tender. Stir in flour until blended. Gradually stir in chicken broth, milk and remaining 2 tablespoons dill weed.

Heat to simmer. Add turkey balls and return to simmer. Cover and simmer 10 minutes.

Push meat balls to side of pan. Add little hot mushroom sauce to remaining 1/4 cup egg substitute to temper. Stir into sauce in pan. Whisk just until slightly thickened, about 1 minute. Remove from heat. Whisk in lemon juice. Add white pepper.

4 servings. Each serving contains about: 171 calories; 874 mg sodium; 59 mg cholesterol; 3 grams fat; 8 grams carbohydrates; 27 grams protein; 0.19 gram fiber.

MEAT, FISH AND POULTRY

Using ground turkey as a replacement for ground beef is a time-honored way to cut fat in favorite recipes. This recipe goes even further; it uses only ground turkey breast, which contains a little less than half the fat of dark turkey meat. If you do not see ground turkey breast in the meat case, ask the butcher to grind it for you.

Serve the turkey meat balls with rice or noodles.

MEAT, FISH AND POULTRY

To keep these low-fat turkey fajitas as quick and easy as possible, buy the turkey breast already cut into strips and ready to stir-fry.

Stir-fry them in a single layer so they will brown quickly without getting watery and steam-cooked; do them in two batches if necessary.

All in all, it takes about 10 minutes to stir-fry the entire dish from beginning to end. Serve the fajitas in small, extra-thin warm tortillas.

TURKEY FAJITAS

NONSTICK COOKING SPRAY
1 POUND TURKEY BREAST STRIPS
4 CLOVES GARLIC, MINCED
1 LARGE ONION, DICED
1 GREEN BELL PEPPER, CUT INTO 1-INCH PIECES
1 SERRANO CHILE, MINCED
2 TOMATOES, DICED
1 CUP MUSHROOMS, SLICED (ABOUT 1/4 POUND)
1/2 TEASPOON CUMIN
SALT
CRUSHED RED PEPPER FLAKES
6 SMALL, EXTRA-THIN CORN TORTILLAS, WARMED
LIME WEDGES
CILANTRO

Spray wok or large skillet with nonstick cooking spray and heat until hot. Add turkey and sauté until lightly browned, 2 to 3 minutes. Remove from pan and keep warm.

Spray pan with nonstick cooking spray and heat until hot. Add garlic, onion, bell pepper and chile. Sauté until vegetables are tender, 3 to 4 minutes.

Add tomatoes and mushrooms and sauté 2 to 3 more minutes. Return meat to wok and heat until hot through. Stir in cumin and season to taste with salt and crushed red pepper.

Spoon filling into warmed tortillas. Fold burrito-style. Serve with lime wedges and cilantro sprigs.

6 servings. Each serving: 128 calories; 116 mg sodium; 33 mg cholesterol; 2 grams fat; 13 grams carbohydrates; 16 grams protein; 1.20 grams fiber.

TURKEY AND VEGETABLE RICE BOWL

1 CLOVE GARLIC, MINCED
1 TEASPOON MINCED GINGER ROOT
1/2 CUP LIGHT SOY SAUCE
1/4 CUP RICE VINEGAR
2 TEASPOONS SUGAR
1/4 TEASPOON SESAME OIL
1/4 TEASPOON CHINESE FIVE-SPICE POWDER
SALT

2 GREEN ONIONS, MINCED
1/2 POUND TURKEY TENDERLOIN
1 CUP SHORT-GRAIN RICE
12 BABY CARROTS, QUARTERED (ABOUT 2 OUNCES)
8 GREEN BEANS, CUT INTO 1/2-INCH PIECES (ABOUT 2 OUNCES)
NONSTICK COOKING SPRAY
2 TEASPOONS CORNSTARCH
CILANTRO LEAVES

Combine garlic, ginger, soy sauce, rice vinegar, sugar, sesame oil, five-spice powder and salt to taste. Stir in onions. Place turkey tenderloin in shallow glass dish with 1/2 soy sauce mixture and marinate several hours to overnight; reserve remaining 1/2 marinade.

Combine rice and 2 cups water in saucepan. Heat to boiling. Reduce heat to simmer, cover and cook 20 minutes. Add carrots and green beans to rice during last 10 minutes of cooking. Let stand covered while grilling turkey.

Remove turkey tenderloins from dish, discarding marinade, and grill on hibachi or stove-top grill sprayed with nonstick cooking spray over medium-high heat until cooked through, 10 to 15 minutes.

Fluff rice with fork. Divide into two large serving bowls. Slice turkey crosswise and arrange on top of rice.

Combine reserved 1/2 marinade with 1/4 cup water in small saucepan. Bring to boil. Blend together cornstarch and 2 teaspoons water until smooth. Stir into saucepan and bring to boil, stirring constantly, until thickened and clear. Spoon sauce over turkey and sprinkle cilantro leaves on top.

2 servings. Each serving: 582 calories; 1,671 mg sodium; 51 mg cholesterol; 3 grams fat; 104 grams carbohydrates; 32 grams protein; 2.46 grams fiber.

MEAT, FISH AND POULTRY

Rice bowls are terrific one-dish meals. This one uses turkey tenderloins that have been marinated, preferably overnight. But if you are pushed for time, marinate the meat just as long as you can.

Start cooking the rice and vegetables before grilling the tenderloins. Then, while the turkey and rice are cooking, thicken the reserved marinade for a sauce; it takes only about a minute.

MEAT, FISH AND POULTRY

Chili is the perfect casual party dish for busy cooks because it can be made a day before serving. In fact, it tastes even better if refrigerated overnight and reheated.

Shortly before guests arrive, put the chili on to simmer gently in a crock pot so people can dip in when they're ready to eat.

The red chile sauce can be found in the Mexican food section of most grocery stores, but check the label to be sure the brand you buy is nonfat. Pasilla chile powder is darker and more flavorful than what you normally find in the spice section.

TURKEY CHILI

- 1 CUP DICED ONION
- 3 CLOVES GARLIC, MINCED
- 2 FRESH LONG GREEN CHILES, SEEDED AND CHOPPED
- NONSTICK COOKING SPRAY
- 1 POUND GROUND TURKEY OR CHICKEN
- 3 TABLESPOONS PASILLA CHILE POWDER OR TO TASTE
- 2 TEASPOONS GROUND CUMIN
- 1 TEASPOON DRIED OREGANO
- 1 TEASPOON SALT
- 1 (1-POUND 10-OUNCE) CAN RED BEANS, SAUCE AND CHIPOTLE PEPPERS
- 1 (1 POUND 12-OUNCE) CAN RED CHILE SAUCE
- 1 (28-OUNCE) CAN WHOLE TOMATOES WITH LIQUID
- 1 (6-OUNCE) CAN TOMATO PASTE
- 2 CUPS WATER
- 1 RED ONION, SLIVERED

Sauté onion, garlic and green chiles in large, heavy saucepan sprayed with nonstick cooking spray until tender. Stir in ground turkey. Sauté, stirring occasionally, until meat loses red color. Stir in chile powder, cumin, oregano and salt. Add red beans, chile sauce, tomatoes with liquid, tomato paste and water. Stir until blended. Bring to boil. Reduce heat and simmer 1 hour. Ladle into bowls and serve with slivered onion.

12 (1-cup) servings. Each serving: 134 calories; 1,228 mg sodium; 18 mg cholesterol; 2 grams fat; 21 grams carbohydrates; 11 grams protein; 4.74 grams fiber.

TURKEY MEAT BALLS IN RED SAUCE

MEAT BALLS
- 1 pound ground turkey
- 1/2 cup nonfat egg substitute (equivalent to 2 eggs)
- 1/2 cup fat-free saltine crackers (about 12 crackers)
- 1/4 cup grated Parmesan cheese
- 2 tablespoons minced onion
- 1 clove garlic, crushed
- 2 tablespoons nonfat milk
- 1 teaspoon salt
- Dash black pepper

RED SAUCE
- Olive oil cooking spray
- 1 large onion, chopped
- 1 clove garlic, chopped
- 2 pounds Roma tomatoes, peeled and diced
- 1 (6-ounce) can tomato paste
- 2 teaspoons dried basil
- 1/2 teaspoon dried oregano
- 2 teaspoons salt
- 1/4 teaspoon black pepper
- 1 quart water

MEAT BALLS
Lightly mix together turkey, egg substitute, crushed crackers, Parmesan cheese, onion, garlic, milk, salt and pepper. Shape into 32 meatballs. Refrigerate, covered, until ready to add to sauce. (They are not browned first.)

RED SAUCE
Spray heavy-bottomed 5-quart Dutch oven with olive oil cooking spray. Add onion and cook until it begins to brown. Add garlic and cook 2 to 3 minutes. Stir in tomatoes, tomato paste, basil, oregano, salt and pepper. Stir in water. Heat to boiling, stirring occasionally. Reduce heat and simmer 30 minutes, stirring. Gently drop meatballs into bubbling sauce. Simmer 30 minutes, stirring occasionally.

8 servings. Each serving: 135 calories; 1,053 mg sodium; 30 mg cholesterol; 3 grams fat; 14 grams carbohydrates; 14 grams protein; 1.05 grams fiber.

MEAT, FISH AND POULTRY

Forget those high-fat meatballs and rich sausages. Ground turkey is leaner and, when cooked in red sauce, has a rich taste. Make this dish a day ahead and it will taste even better.

Adding water to the tomatoes is an old trick that gives you a smooth sauce that is ample enough for cooking the meatballs.

Serve the meat balls and sauce over spaghetti or rice.

You may have had fried tofu with spicy minced pork in Chinese restaurants. This version cuts way back on the fat by using ground turkey and a non-traditional frying technique.

Usually when you fry tofu, you dip it in egg and then in cornstarch before frying in hot oil. Here, you can simply pat a small amount of cornstarch onto the tofu to coat it, then brown it in a hot skillet sprayed with nonfat cooking spray.

Be sure to pick the firm variety, which holds up best for frying.

ASIAN MINCED TURKEY WITH TOFU

NONSTICK COOKING SPRAY
4 CLOVES GARLIC, MINCED
2 TABLESPOONS MINCED GINGER ROOT
1 POUND EXTRA-LEAN GROUND TURKEY
1 1/2 CUPS NONFAT CHICKEN BROTH
6 TABLESPOONS SOY SAUCE
3 TABLESPOONS RICE WINE VINEGAR
1 1/2 TABLESPOONS HOISIN SAUCE
1 TEASPOON HOT CHILE SAUCE
1/4 CUP CORNSTARCH
2 TABLESPOONS WATER
1 TEASPOON SESAME OIL
2 GREEN ONIONS, SLICED
2 (10 1/2-OUNCE) PACKAGES FIRM LOW-FAT TOFU, WELL-DRAINED
CHOPPED CILANTRO

Heat wok or heavy skillet over very high heat. Spray hot wok with cooking spray. Add garlic and ginger and sauté quickly. Add turkey and sauté, breaking up meat into small pieces.

When meat is browned, stir in chicken broth, soy sauce, vinegar, hoisin sauce and chile sauce. Bring to boil; reduce heat and simmer 5 minutes to blend flavors.

Blend 2 tablespoons cornstarch and water until smooth. Stir into simmering turkey mixture. Add sesame oil and heat to boiling. Cook and stir until mixture is thickened and clear. Stir in onions. Keep warm while preparing tofu.

Cut each package of tofu into 3 lengthwise slices. Pat slices dry with paper towel. Rub each side of each slice of tofu with 1/2 teaspoon cornstarch. Spray hot skillet with cooking spray and cook tofu until browned on one side, about 2 minutes, then turn to brown second side. To serve, spoon hot minced turkey over tofu and sprinkle with chopped cilantro.

6 servings. Each serving: 162 calories; 1,657 mg sodium; 34 mg cholesterol; 3 grams fat; 10 grams carbohydrates; 22 grams protein; 0.16 gram fiber.

CHICKEN ENCHILADAS

- 1 (1-POUND 13-OUNCE) CAN ENCHILADA SAUCE
- 8 CORN TORTILLAS
- 3 CUPS SHREDDED COOKED CHICKEN BREAST MEAT, SKIN REMOVED
- 3 GREEN ONIONS, MINCED
- 2 CANNED WHOLE LONG GREEN CHILES, CUT INTO QUARTERS LENGTHWISE
- 1/2 CUP LOW-FAT MONTEREY JACK CHEESE
- 2 TABLESPOONS CHOPPED CILANTRO
- 1/4 CUP PLAIN NONFAT YOGURT OR NONFAT SOUR CREAM

Heat enchilada sauce in skillet until hot. Dip tortillas, 1 at time, in sauce to coat lightly on both sides. Sprinkle about 1/3 cup chicken down center of each tortilla. Sprinkle with 2 teaspoons onion, then top with 1 piece chile. Roll up and place, seam-side down, in 9-inch square baking dish. Repeat with remaining tortillas.

Pour remaining enchilada sauce over top of tortillas. Sprinkle with cheese. Bake at 400 degrees until hot and cheese is melted, 20 to 25 minutes. Just before serving, sprinkle with chopped cilantro. Serve with yogurt.

4 servings. Each serving, with yogurt topping: 443 calories; 1,215 mg sodium; 99 mg cholesterol; 10 grams fat; 36 grams carbohydrates; 40 grams protein; 0.04 gram fiber.

MEAT, FISH AND POULTRY

These chicken enchiladas contain just 10 grams of fat per serving compared to 37 grams in a traditional recipe.

Here are some of the tricks I used. To soften the tortillas, dip them in the warm enchilada sauce right away, rather than frying them in oil first (the traditional way). Also, use poached, skinless chicken breast meat for the filling instead of dark meat. Low-fat Jack cheese contains half the fat of regular Jack cheese. And nonfat yogurt tops the enchiladas instead of sour cream.

Vegetables and Other Side Dishes

This is the sort of rich, creamy side dish that is served most often during the holidays. The difference is that nonfat milk and flour make the cream, which significantly reduces the dish's fat count and your guilt.

To cut the fat even more, use nonstick cooking spray instead of butter to grease the pan and toast the bread crumbs.

When fresh Brussels sprouts on the stalk are in season, you can wrap the entire stalk in plastic and store it in the refrigerator for up to a week. Break off just as many sprouts as you need, while storing the rest.

BRUSSELS SPROUTS IN GARLIC CREAM SAUCE

1 WHOLE HEAD GARLIC
NONSTICK OLIVE OIL COOKING SPRAY
COARSE SALT
1 POUND BRUSSELS SPROUTS
1 TABLESPOON MINCED SHALLOTS
6 TABLESPOONS FLOUR
1 1/2 CUPS NONFAT CHICKEN BROTH
1 1/2 CUPS NONFAT MILK
1/2 TEASPOON SALT
1/8 TEASPOON WHITE PEPPER
1 TABLESPOON BUTTER, PLUS EXTRA FOR GREASING DISH
1 CUP FRESH BREAD CRUMBS

Cut top off stem end of garlic head. Place, cut side up, on square piece of foil large enough to wrap around garlic. Spray garlic with olive oil cooking spray and season with coarse salt to taste. Fold foil over garlic and seal ends. Roast at 400 degrees until garlic is tender, about 30 minutes. Remove from oven and let cool.

Quarter large Brussels sprouts and halve smaller ones. Steam in steamer until tender, about 15 minutes.

Lightly spray small saucepan with cooking spray. Add shallots and sauté over low heat, stirring constantly, until shallots are tender and begin to brown, 1 to 2 minutes. Remove from heat and stir in flour. Gradually add chicken broth and stir until smooth and blended. Stir in milk, salt and white pepper. Bring to boil over medium heat, stirring constantly. Boil and stir until sauce is thickened, about 1 minute.

Squeeze 6 cloves roasted garlic from skin and press through garlic press into sauce, whisking until blended. Stir in steamed Brussels sprouts.

Spoon into lightly buttered 1 1/2-quart baking dish. Melt 1 tablespoon butter in small skillet over low heat. Add bread crumbs and lightly brown over low heat, stirring constantly, 1 to 2 minutes. Spoon bread crumbs over top of casserole. Bake at 400 degrees until hot and bubbly, 20 to 25 minutes.

6 servings. Each serving: 136 calories; 405 mg sodium; 7 mg cholesterol; 3 grams fat; 21 grams carbohydrates; 8 grams protein; 1.15 grams fiber.

HUNGARIAN-STYLE CREAMED YELLOW BEANS

- 4 CLOVES GARLIC, MINCED
- NONSTICK COOKING SPRAY
- 1 POUND YELLOW WAX BEANS OR GREEN BEANS, CUT INTO 2-INCH PIECES
- WATER
- 1 1/2 CUPS NONFAT MILK
- 2 TEASPOONS SUGAR
- 1 TABLESPOON MINCED DILL
- 1/2 TEASPOON SALT
- 1 1/2 TABLESPOONS FLOUR
- 1 TABLESPOON WHITE VINEGAR

Sauté garlic in small skillet sprayed with nonstick cooking spray until tender, 1 to 2 minutes, stirring frequently. Set aside.

Add yellow beans to boiling water in saucepan. Water should just barely cover beans. Cover and simmer until beans are crisp and barely tender, about 10 minutes. Drain beans.

Add milk, sugar, dill, salt and sautéed garlic to beans. Bring to boil. Blend together flour and 2 tablespoons water until smooth. Stir into boiling milk until slightly thickened. Reduce heat to simmer and continue to cook until thickened and flavors blend, about 10 minutes. Stir in vinegar.

4 servings. Each serving: 95 calories; 357 mg sodium; 2 mg cholesterol; 0 fat; 19 grams carbohydrates; 6 grams protein; 1.30 grams fiber.

VEGETABLES AND OTHER SIDE DISHES

Yellow beans with dill, *kapros sárgababfőzelék,* is a traditional Hungarian dish that has an unusual sweet-and-sour cream sauce made with a touch of vinegar and sugar.

Traditionally, the creamy texture comes from combining bacon fat and cream. Here they've been replaced by a bit of flour and nonfat milk.

Sautéing the garlic before adding it to the sauce gives a smoother flavor to the dish.

VEGETABLES AND OTHER SIDE DISHES

The sweet-tart flavor of reduced balsamic vinegar with the scent of thyme is a great match for roasted acorn squash.

Don't throw away any extra toasted squash seeds; they make a great crunchy snack.

BALSAMIC ROASTED SQUASH WITH TOASTED SQUASH SEEDS

1/4 CUP BALSAMIC VINEGAR
1 CUP NONFAT LOW-SODIUM CHICKEN BROTH
FEW SPRIGS THYME
2 (1- TO 1 1/4-POUND) ACORN SQUASH, HALVED
NONSTICK COOKING SPRAY
SALT, PEPPER

Combine vinegar, broth and thyme. Bring to boil, then reduce heat and simmer until liquid is reduced to about 1/3 cup, about 15 minutes.

Remove seeds from squash and set aside for toasting. Arrange squash cut-side up in single layer on baking pan sprayed with nonstick cooking spray. Season to taste with salt and pepper and brush with balsamic sauce.

Roast at 425 degrees until tender, 35 to 45 minutes. Brush squash with balsamic mixture several times during roasting.

Meanwhile, place squash seeds in strainer and rinse off fibers under cold running water. Pat seeds dry, then scatter in single layer on baking sheet sprayed with nonstick cooking spray. Lightly spray seeds with cooking spray, then roast at 350 degrees until they are lightly browned, 15 to 20 minutes. Season to taste with salt.

Remove squash from oven and sprinkle with toasted squash seeds before serving.

4 servings. Each serving: 108 calories; 123 mg sodium; 0 cholesterol; 0 fat; 26 grams carbohydrates; 4 grams protein; 3.17 grams fiber.

VEGETABLES AND OTHER SIDE DISHES

SAVORY BAKED SWEET POTATOES

4 SWEET POTATOES, ABOUT 3/4 POUND EACH
1 BUNCH FRESH ROSEMARY
8 TO 12 THIN SLICES GARLIC
NONSTICK COOKING SPRAY
KOSHER SALT
CRACKED BLACK PEPPER

Clean sweet potatoes under running water and pat dry. Make deep crosswise cuts about every inch, 2 to 3 cuts per potato; cut almost but not quite through, leaving potatoes intact. Insert several sprigs rosemary and few slices garlic deep into cuts.

Place on baking sheet and spray potatoes with cooking spray. Sprinkle with kosher salt and pepper to taste. Bake at 375 degrees just until potatoes are tender and lightly browned, about 1 hour.

Makes 4 servings. Each serving: 319 calories; 98 mg sodium; 0 cholesterol; 0 fat; 75 grams carbohydrates; 4 grams protein; 2.71 grams fiber.

Select sweet potatoes that are about the same size. They should be the sweet, moist dark-skinned type with orange flesh, not the pale or yellow variety. The potatoes are sliced deeply and baked with the garlic and rosemary in the cuts. After about an hour, the potatoes and the tips of the rosemary sprigs will be browned and full of flavor.

HERB ROASTED POTATOES AND PEPPERS

NONSTICK OLIVE OIL COOKING SPRAY
3 BAKING POTATOES, CUT LENGTHWISE INTO 8 WEDGES
1 RED BELL PEPPER, CUT INTO QUARTERS LENGTHWISE AND SEEDED
1 YELLOW BELL PEPPER, CUT INTO QUARTERS LENGTHWISE AND SEEDED
1 GREEN BELL PEPPER, CUT INTO QUARTERS LENGTHWISE AND SEEDED
1 TABLESPOON COARSELY CHOPPED ROSEMARY
4 CLOVES GARLIC, MINCED
KOSHER SALT
CRACKED BLACK PEPPER
1 LEMON, CUT IN HALF

Spray large baking pan with olive oil cooking spray. Arrange potatoes and red, yellow and green bell peppers in single layer on baking pan. Spray lightly with olive oil cooking spray. Sprinkle with rosemary and garlic. Season with salt and cracked black pepper to taste. Bake at 425 degrees until vegetables are tender and browned, 35 to 45 minutes. Squeeze lemon over all just before serving.

Makes 6 servings. Each serving contains about: 72 calories; 55 mg sodium; 0 cholesterol; 0 fat; 18 grams carbohydrates; 2 grams protein; 0.41 gram fiber.

The peppers are cut into quarters so the roasting time is about the same as for the potato wedges.

The seasonings in this recipe are rosemary, garlic, salt and pepper, but you may use other flavorings according to your taste. To maximize flavor, lightly spray the vegetables with the flavored cooking spray after arranging them on the baking pan.

VEGETABLES AND OTHER SIDE DISHES

This traditional Central European dish, called *kelkaposzta fozelek*, is a delicious vegetable stew of savoy cabbage, potatoes and seasonings.

For maximum flavor with minimal fat, this version of the recipe uses nonfat chicken broth, rather than water or a high-fat meat stock. Also for maximum flavor, a minimum amount of butter or non-fat cooking spray is used in the sautéing.

Kelkaposzta fozelek is delicious served with a dollop of nonfat sour cream and a sprinkle of Hungarian paprika.

And don't worry about any leftovers; this dish tastes even better the second day.

CABBAGE AND POTATOES

1 ONION, DICED
3 CLOVES GARLIC, MINCED
2 TABLESPOONS BUTTER OR NON-FAT COOKING SPRAY
1 (2-POUND) HEAD SAVOY CABBAGE, SHREDDED
3 (14-1/2 OUNCE) CANS FAT-FREE CHICKEN BROTH
2 BAKING POTATOES, PEELED AND CUBED
1 TEASPOON PAPRIKA
1/4 TEASPOON GROUND CUMIN
SALT, PEPPER
1 TABLESPOON FLOUR
CHOPPED PARSLEY

In large saucepan sauté onion and garlic in 1 tablespoon butter until tender. Add shredded cabbage. Cook and stir until cabbage is just tender. Add chicken broth. Bring to boil. Reduce heat, cover and simmer 30 minutes. Add potatoes, paprika and cumin. Season to taste with salt and pepper. Cover and simmer 30 minutes.

Blend together remaining 1 tablespoon butter and flour in small bowl. Blend into bubbling liquid. Cook and stir until liquid thickens slightly. To serve, spoon into large flat bowl and garnish with parsley. Makes 8 servings.

Each serving contains: 107 calories; 536 mg sodium; 8 mg cholesterol; 4 grams fat; 16 grams carbohydrates; 5 grams protein; 1.23 grams fiber.

EGGPLANT STACK

4 (1/2-INCH-THICK) SLICES EGGPLANT

1/4 CUP SHREDDED NONFAT MOZZARELLA CHEESE

1/2 POUND BROWN MUSHROOMS, SLICED

2 CLOVES GARLIC, MINCED

NONSTICK OLIVE OIL COOKING SPRAY

1 TEASPOON CHOPPED OREGANO LEAVES

1 TEASPOON CHOPPED BASIL LEAVES

SALT, PEPPER

8 THIN SLICES ROMA TOMATOES

2 OUNCES FRESH NONFAT MOZZARELLA CHEESE, CUT INTO 4 THIN SLICES

8 BASIL LEAVES, CUT INTO THIN STRIPS CROSSWISE

Brown slices of eggplant in hot skillet over medium-high heat until browned on both sides, 3 to 5 minutes per side. Remove to baking pan.

Top each eggplant slice with 1 tablespoon shredded mozzarella cheese.

Sauté mushrooms and garlic, in skillet sprayed with nonstick cooking spray, until tender. Stir in chopped oregano and basil. Season to taste with salt and pepper.

Divide and spoon mushrooms over eggplant slices. Top each with 2 slices tomato, then slices of fresh mozzarella cheese. Bake at 375 degrees until eggplant is hot throughout and cheese is melted, about 15 minutes. Sprinkle with strips of basil and serve.

Makes 4 servings. Each serving contains about: 84 calories; 190 mg sodium; 11 mg cholesterol; 4 grams fat; 6 grams carbohydrates; 7 grams protein; 0.74 gram fiber.

VEGETABLES AND OTHER SIDE DISHES

If you "dry-fry" eggplant with no oil, it comes out beautifully browned, ready to be cooked further in stews or to eat topped with melted nonfat mozzarella cheese, tomatoes, mushrooms and herbs. The technique is a terrific alternative to regular oil frying if you're making eggplant Parmesan.

There's no need to salt and drain the eggplant before cooking when you use this method, but be sure the skillet is hot before adding the eggplant slices.

VEGETABLES AND OTHER SIDE DISHES

Chayotes are easy to prepare for stuffing. Pick small, pear-shaped chayotes that are firm and dark green in color. After cooking them in boiling water until tender, cut them in half lengthwise. Remove the single flat seed.

Next, use a small knife to cut around the edges and remove the flesh. Be careful not to puncture the skins.

After baking, spoon the tomato mixture from the bottom of the baking dish over the top of each stuffed squash. The squash should be tender enough to cut through with ease.

STUFFED CHAYOTE SQUASH

2 CHAYOTE SQUASH
2 LARGE TOMATOES
NONSTICK COOKING SPRAY
1/2 CUP MINCED ONION
1 CLOVE GARLIC, MINCED
1/2 CUP SHORT-GRAIN RICE
1 (14 1/2-OUNCE) CAN NONFAT CHICKEN BROTH
1/2 TEASPOON PAPRIKA
1 TABLESPOONS MINCED FRESH MARJORAM
SALT, PEPPER
GRATED PARMESAN CHEESE

Cook squash in boiling water to cover until tender, 20 to 25 minutes. Drain and cut in half. Remove seeds and scoop flesh from shell, being careful not to cut through skins. Chop squash meat and set aside. Reserve skins.

Cut tomatoes in half and grate in bowl, discarding skin. Spray skillet with nonstick cooking spray. Add onion and sauté 2 to 3 minutes. Add garlic and cook until onion is almost tender, about 2 more minutes. Stir in rice.

Combine 3/4 cup broth and 1/2 cup grated tomato and set aside. Add remaining broth and tomato to rice. Simmer, stirring occasionally, until rice is partly cooked and liquid is absorbed but rice is not dry, 8 to 10 minutes. Stir in reserved chopped squash, paprika, marjoram and salt and pepper to taste.

Season squash shells with salt and pepper to taste. Spoon rice into shells. Arrange stuffed squash in 9-inch square baking dish. Pour reserved tomato-broth mixture around squash. Cover and bake at 350 degrees until rice is cooked through, 45 to 60 minutes.

Remove from oven and spoon tomato mixture from bottom of baking dish over top of each stuffed squash. Sprinkle Parmesan cheese over tops.

Makes 4 stuffed halves. Each serving contains about: 148 calories; 376 mg sodium; 0 cholesterol; 1 gram fat; 31 grams carbohydrates; 4 grams protein; 1.39 grams fiber.

VEGETARIAN HUNGARIAN LECSO

NONSTICK MESQUITE COOKING SPRAY

1 TABLESPOON CANOLA OIL

1 LARGE ONION, DICED

1 TABLESPOON SWEET HUNGARIAN PAPRIKA

3 LARGE TOMATOES, PEELED AND CUT INTO WEDGES (ABOUT 1 1/2 POUNDS)

6 TO 7 HUNGARIAN PEPPERS, SEEDED AND CUT INTO 1-INCH STRIPS (ABOUT 1 POUND)

1 TEASPOON SALT

TOMATO RICE

Spray bottom of Dutch oven with mesquite cooking spray. Add oil and heat until hot. Add onion and sauté over medium heat until onion turns brown around edges, 3 to 4 minutes. Remove from heat and stir in paprika. Reduce heat to low.

Stir in tomato wedges, pepper strips and salt. Cover and cook over low heat until tomatoes cook down to gravy and peppers are limp, 25 to 30 minutes. Stir occasionally. Correct seasoning, if necessary. Serve with Tomato Rice.

Makes 4 servings. Each serving, without Tomato Rice, contains about: 102 calories; 605 mg sodium; 0 cholesterol; 4 grams fat; 16 grams carbohydrates; 3 grams protein; 1.83 gram fiber.

TOMATO RICE

1 CUP RICE

2 CUPS WATER

1 TEASPOON SALT

NONSTICK COOKING SPRAY

1 SMALL ONION, MINCED

1 CLOVE GARLIC, MINCED

1 TOMATO, DICED

Combine rice, water and salt in saucepan. Heat to boiling. Reduce heat, cover and simmer until rice is tender and water is absorbed, 20 to 25 minutes.

Spray skillet with nonstick cooking spray. Add onion, garlic and tomato and sauté until tender. Stir into cooked rice.

Makes 4 servings. Each serving contains about: 183 calories; 595 mg sodium; 0 cholesterol; 0 fat; 41 grams carbohydrates; 4 grams protein; 0.45 gram fiber.

VEGETABLES AND OTHER SIDE DISHES

Lecsó (pronounced LETCH-o) is a savory stew or sauce of tomatoes and Hungarian peppers. Traditionally, it's flavored with smoked bacon, but this low-fat vegetarian version gets its smokiness from mesquite cooking spray.

For a really great *lecso*, you'll need garden-fresh tomatoes because juices from the simmering tomatoes and peppers are needed to form a rich, red, gravy-like sauce. If the tomatoes aren't ripe, they won't be juicy enough to make the sauce, and you may need to add water or chicken broth.

Long, pale green Hungarian peppers are often available at supermarkets and farmers' markets, but in a pinch you could substitute bell peppers.

VEGETABLES AND OTHER SIDE DISHES

Coconut milk is a must in Thai curry sauces, but it is high in fat. However, the new light coconut milk now available in Thai and ethnic foods sections of most supermarkets means that you can have a great curry with about half the fat.

To give your sauce a creamy consistency that will cling to the rice, thicken it with a little flour. You can find the yellow curry paste that gives this dish its golden color in most Thai markets. Serve the curry with brown rice as a main dish or as a side dish with poultry, meat or seafood.

VEGETABLE CURRY

1/2 ONION, THINLY SLICED
NONSTICK COOKING SPRAY
2 CLOVES GARLIC, MINCED
1 TEASPOON YELLOW CURRY PASTE
1 (14 1/2-OUNCE) CAN NONFAT CHICKEN BROTH
1 SMALL CARROT, SLICED
2 WHITE ROSE POTATOES, PEELED AND DICED
1 (14-OUNCE) CAN LIGHT COCONUT MILK
1 TABLESPOON FLOUR
1 TABLESPOON WATER
1/2 CUP FROZEN GREEN PEAS
BROWN RICE

Sauté onion in skillet sprayed with nonstick cooking spray until browned around edges, 3 to 4 minutes. Add garlic and cook 1 minute. Add curry paste and sauté about 30 seconds.

Stir in chicken broth and bring to simmer. Add carrot and potatoes and simmer until tender, about 15 minutes. Stir in coconut milk.

Blend together flour and water until smooth. Stir into curry. Bring to boil and stir until thickened, about 1 minute. Add peas and stir until hot through, 1 to 2 minutes. Serve with brown rice.

6 main-course or 8 side-dish servings. Each main-course serving: 115 calories; 300 mg sodium; 0 cholesterol; 6 grams fat; 10 grams carbohydrates; 4 grams protein; 0.56 gram fiber.

PILAF WITH ASSORTED VEGETABLES

Nonstick cooking spray

1/2 cup minced onion

3 cloves garlic, minced

1/2 pound mushrooms, chopped

1 (1 pound, 3 1/2-ounce) box seven whole grains and sesame pilaf, about 2 cups

2 cups water

2 cups chicken broth

2 teaspoon salt

1 (15 1/2-ounce) can garbanzo beans, drained and rinsed

3/4 pound broccoli florets, steamed

2 large carrots, peeled, sliced diagonally and steamed

2 tablespoons coarsely chopped basil

Spray large saucepan with nonstick cooking spray. Add onion and garlic and sauté until onion begins to brown, about 3 to 4 minutes. Add mushrooms and continue to cook until mushrooms are tender, about 5 minutes. Stir in pilaf mix and cook until grains are lightly toasted, several minutes.

Add water, broth and salt. Bring to boil, reduce heat to medium, cover and simmer just until water is absorbed, 25 to 30 minutes. Stir in garbanzo beans and steamed broccoli and carrots. Stir in chopped basil.

Makes 8 servings. Each serving contains about: 362 calories; 990 mg sodium; 0 cholesterol; 6 grams fat; 64 grams carbohydrates; 15 grams protein; 10.70 grams fiber.

Vegetables and Other Side Dishes

This pilaf of fresh vegetables, garbanzo beans and nutty grains makes a hearty, satisfying meal that is low in fat, high in fiber.

It relies on Kashi pilaf mix, available in the breakfast foods and cereal section of many grocery stores and health food stores.

If you have trouble finding it, substitute a combination of equal quantities whole oats, long-grain brown rice, whole rye, whole hard red winter wheat, whole triticale, whole buckwheat, whole barley and sesame seeds. The cooking time, however, must be increased if you do this. You can also try seven-grain cereal, sold in many health food stores.

VEGETABLES AND OTHER SIDE DISHES

This is no ordinary diet-plate stuffed tomato, and you won't feel deprived.

Eggplant, which gives meatless dishes a feeling of substance, goes into the rice stuffing. To give the filling a smoky, earthy flavor, leave the charred skins on the roasted eggplants when you add them to the stuffing.

STUFFED TOMATOES

2 Japanese eggplants
6 large, firm tomatoes
Salt, pepper
1 tablespoon olive oil
1/2 cup minced onion
2 cloves garlic, minced
1 cup short-grain rice
2/3 cup chicken broth
1/4 cup minced basil
6 basil leaves

Grill eggplants over open flame or under broiler until skin is blistered all over, eggplant smells roasted and interior is soft. Remove stems. Chop and set aside.

Remove tops from tomatoes. Scoop out insides, leaving 1/2-inch shell. Purée pulp through food mill, discarding seeds left behind. Season inside of tomatoes to taste with salt and pepper.

Heat oil in skillet and sauté onion and garlic in skillet until tender. Add rice and continue to sauté until lightly browned. Stir in 1/2 cup chicken broth and all but 1/2 cup tomato pulp. Simmer until rice is partially cooked, 8 to 10 minutes. Stir in minced basil and reserved eggplant. Season to taste with salt and pepper.

Spoon rice mixture into shells. Top each with whole basil leaf. Replace tops. Place in 3-quart rectangular baking dish. Combine remaining broth and reserved pulp. Pour around tomatoes. Lightly season tomatoes to taste with salt. Bake at 350 degrees 45 minutes to 1 hour or until rice and tomatoes are tender. Spoon juices over tomatoes while baking. Serve warm, at room temperature or cold. Makes 6 servings.

Each serving contains about: 180 calories; 148 mg sodium; trace cholesterol; 3 grams fat; 35 grams carbohydrates; 4 grams protein; 1.08 grams fiber.

SWEET-AND-SOUR TOFU

1 POUND FIRM TOFU
NONSTICK COOKING SPRAY
3 TABLESPOONS CORNSTARCH
3/4 CUP SUGAR
1/4 CUP RICE VINEGAR
1/4 CUP CATSUP
1 1/4 CUPS WATER
1/4 CUP PINEAPPLE JUICE
1 CLOVE GARLIC, THINLY SLICED
1 TEASPOON SLIVERED GINGER
1 GREEN BELL PEPPER, CUT INTO 1 1/2-INCH SQUARES
1 TOMATO, CUT INTO THIN WEDGES AND SEEDED

Drain tofu and pat dry with paper towels. Cut into 1-inch cubes and drain on paper towels, patting off excess moisture.

Spray skillet with nonstick cooking spray and heat over medium-high heat. Add cubed tofu to hot skillet and sauté until browned on all sides, turning as necessary. Remove from heat and keep warm.

Combine cornstarch and sugar in saucepan. Stir in vinegar and catsup until smooth. Stir in water and pineapple juice until blended, then add garlic and ginger. Heat and stir until boiling. Reduce heat to simmer and stir until thickened and clear, 1 to 2 minutes. Keep warm.

Blanch bell pepper squares in hot water until they turn bright green, about 1 minute. Drain and stir into hot sweet-and-sour sauce along with tomato and tofu and bring to boil. Simmer an additional 1 to 2 minutes.

6 servings. Each serving: 188 calories; 186 mg sodium; 0 cholesterol; 1 gram fat; 40 grams carbohydrates; 6 grams protein; 0.44 gram fiber.

VEGETABLES AND OTHER SIDE DISHES

The sweet-and-sour flavors that many of us grew up with give a nostalgic twist to this vegetarian tofu dish.

For this recipe, be sure to use firm tofu so it won't fall apart when stirred into the sauce.

It is important to drain the block of tofu on paper towels before cutting it into cubes; also drain the cut-up cubes on paper towels and pat them dry to remove any excess moisture so the sauce doesn't thin out.

Serve the tofu with Jasmine rice or brown rice.

[Desserts]

The spectacular cranberry color of the ice and its clean, tart flavor make this a wonderful dessert for sophisticated palates.

The ice may be prepared a few days in advance. If you don't have an ice cream freezer, pour the cranberry mixture into a glass loaf dish and freeze, stirring several times as it freezes. Be sure to cover tightly with foil after the final stirring. Allow the ice to stand at room temperature about 15 minutes before serving for ease in spooning and to bring out the flavor of the fruit.

Note: The cranberries used in the garnish are coated in egg white that is left uncooked. To prevent food-borne illnesses that can result from uncooked eggs, use commercial liquid egg whites sold in most grocery stores.

CRANBERRY ICE

1 (12-OUNCE) PACKAGE FRESH CRANBERRIES OR FROZEN
1 CUP SUGAR
4 CUPS WATER
1/2 CUP RASPBERRY WINE OR RASPBERRY LIQUEUR
SUGARED CRANBERRIES
MINT LEAVES

Rinse cranberries, removing any soft bruised berries. Drain.

Combine cranberries, sugar and water in large saucepan. Bring to boil. Boil 5 minutes, stirring occasionally. Remove from heat and cool to room temperature. Pour through fine mesh strainer, pressing to extract as much juice as possible from berries. Discard berries. Stir in wine.

Freeze mixture in ice cream maker according to manufacturer's instructions. Spoon ice into chilled loaf dish. Cover and freeze until serving time.

To serve, spoon into serving glass or bowl. Garnish each serving with Sugared Cranberries and mint leaves.

10 servings. Each serving: 130 calories; 22 mg sodium; trace cholesterol; trace fat; 30 grams carbohydrates; 2 grams protein; 0.58 gram fiber.

SUGARED CRANBERRIES

FRESH CRANBERRIES
LIGHTLY BEATEN EGG WHITE OR COMMERCIAL LIQUID EGG WHITE
SUGAR

Rinse cranberries and pat dry with paper towels. Dip in lightly beaten egg white. Then roll in granulated sugar to coat. Remove to wire rack. Let stand until sugar dries and hardens.

HONEYDEW ICE

3 CUPS PURÉED HONEYDEW MELON

1 1/2 TABLESPOONS LIME JUICE

1 1/2 TABLESPOONS SUGAR

1/2 CUP HONEYDEW MELON LIQUEUR

4 SLICES LIME, OPTIONAL

4 SLICES BLOOD ORANGE, OPTIONAL

4 SPRIGS MINT, OPTIONAL

Combine honeydew purée, lime juice, sugar and liqueur. Freeze in ice cream freezer according to manufacturer's instructions. (Note: If making ahead, spoon into chilled loaf pan, cover and freeze. Remove from freezer 10 to 15 minutes before serving.)

Spoon into serving glasses and garnish each with slice of lime and slice of blood orange. Top with sprig of mint.

4 servings. Each serving: 203 calories; 14 mg sodium; 0 cholesterol; 0 fat; 20 grams carbohydrates; 1 gram protein; 0.88 gram fiber.

It's cool, it's refreshing and it takes just 30 minutes to make from start to finish. The melon liqueur smooths out the ice, adding sweetness and giving it a bright green color. Be sure to taste the puréed fruit before adding the other ingredients. Depending on the sweetness of the fruit, you may want to use more or less sugar than called for in the recipe.

DESSERTS

Horchata, the cinnamon-scented rice drink from Mexico, gives this ice a soothing, gently spiced flavor. On the side, serve cinnamon-sugar-dusted tortilla crisps instead of cookies.

Note that *horchata* is a nondairy product. It's commonly found in health food stores and in Chinese and Mexican markets.

A tip: Buy an extra bottle of *horchata* and pour it over your breakfast cereal; it's delicious and there's no need to add sugar; a few slices of banana or fresh berries will do.

MEXICAN CHOCOLATE ICE

3 (12-OUNCE) BOTTLES NONDAIRY RICE DRINK (HORCHATA)

1/2 CUP COCOA

1 TEASPOON VANILLA EXTRACT

Combine 1 cup rice drink and cocoa in small saucepan. Heat and stir until cocoa is dissolved. Stir in remaining rice drink and vanilla. Let cool, then freeze in ice cream maker according to manufacturer's directions.

8 servings. Each serving: 551 calories; 121 mg sodium; 0 cholesterol; 7 grams fat; 102 grams carbohydrates; 4 grams protein; 0.30 gram fiber.

TORTILLA CRISPS

4 CORN TORTILLAS

NONSTICK COOKING SPRAY

1 TEASPOON SUGAR

1/4 TEASPOON CINNAMON

POWDERED SUGAR

Cut each tortilla into 8 wedges. Arrange in single layer on baking sheets. Lightly spray with nonstick cooking spray.

Combine sugar and cinnamon, then sprinkle over tortilla wedges. Bake at 400 degrees until chips are brown and crisp, about 10 minutes. Remove from oven and sprinkle with powdered sugar.

Garnish for 8 servings. Each serving: 36 calories; 27 mg sodium; 0 cholesterol; 1 gram fat; 7 grams carbohydrates; 1 gram protein; 0.50 gram fiber.

DATE BITES

- 1 1/2 CUPS CUT-UP PITTED DATES
- 1/2 CUP WATER
- 1/2 CUP SUGAR
- 2 TABLESPOONS LEMON JUICE
- 1/2 TEASPOON VANILLA EXTRACT
- 1/2 CUP OVEN-TOASTED RICE CEREAL
- 8 SHEETS FILO DOUGH
- BUTTER-FLAVORED NONSTICK COOKING SPRAY
- MELTED BUTTER
- POWDERED SUGAR

Combine dates, water and sugar. Bring to boil, stirring occasionally. Boil and stir 5 minutes or until mixture mounds. Stir in lemon juice. Cool to room temperature. Stir in vanilla and rice cereal.

For triangle shapes, spray 1 sheet filo dough with butter-flavored nonstick cooking spray. Top with second sheet of filo and spray again. Cut into 6 strips crosswise. Cut each strip in half to make 12 strips.

Spoon scant 1 teaspoon date filling at top corner of each strip. Fold up "flag" style to make triangle. Place on baking sheets. Lightly brush tops of each with melted butter. Bake at 375 degrees 5 to 6 minutes until lightly browned. Remove to wire rack to cool. Sprinkle with powdered sugar.

About 4 dozen pastries. Each pastry: 36 calories; 15 mg sodium; 1 mg cholesterol; trace fat; 9 grams carbohydrates; 0 protein; 0.12 gram fiber.

DESSERTS

The fat normally contained in these cookies was dramatically reduced by spraying the sheets of filo dough with butter-flavored cooking spray. Real butter is added as a final touch just before the pastries are put into the oven, which gives them a buttery bite but does not add a lot of fat.

The date filling also contains no fat. The trick? The kind of crunchiness that nuts would normally provide comes from puffed rice cereal. In all, each pastry has less than 1 gram of fat.

Note: For date logs, use same procedure as above, cutting filo dough crosswise into 8 strips. Cut each strip in half to make 16 and roll up in log shape.

DESSERTS

Raisins aren't the only fruit that can go in an oatmeal cookie. Dried cherries—and during the holidays dried cranberries—taste terrific and add jewel-like drops of color.

CHEWY OATMEAL-CHERRY COOKIES

1/2 CUP NONFAT EGG SUBSTITUTE (EQUIVALENT TO 2 EGGS)

1 CUP DARK BROWN SUGAR, PACKED

1/2 CUP GRANULATED SUGAR

2 TABLESPOONS NONFAT MILK

1 TABLESPOON BUTTER, SOFTENED

1 TEASPOON VANILLA EXTRACT

1 1/2 CUPS ROLLED OATS

1 CUP FLOUR

1 TEASPOON BAKING SODA

1 TEASPOON SALT

1 1/2 CUPS DRIED CHERRIES

Combine egg substitute, brown sugar, granulated sugar, nonfat milk, butter and vanilla.

Grind 1 1/4 cups of rolled oats in food processor or blender to consistency of flour and combine with flour, baking soda and salt. Stir into sugar-egg mixture. Stir in remaining 1/4 cup rolled oats and cherries. Drop by tablespoons onto greased baking sheets.

Bake at 375 degrees about 5 minutes or until center tests done. Remove from baking sheets while warm to wire rack to cool.

About 4 dozen cookies. Each cookie: 49 calories; 57 mg sodium; 1 mg cholesterol; trace fat; 11 grams carbohydrates; 1 gram protein; 0.05 gram fiber.

The fresh taste of lemon combines with a vanilla wafer crust to make a great-tasting cookie bar with only 2 grams of fat.

After baking, let the pan cool to room temperature before attempting to cut.

LEMON BARS

2 CUPS VANILLA WAFERS, CRUSHED

2 TABLESPOONS BUTTER, MELTED

1/2 CUP NONFAT EGG SUBSTITUTE (EQUIVALENT TO 2 EGGS)

3/4 CUP SUGAR

GRATED ZEST OF 1 LEMON

1/4 CUP LEMON JUICE

DASH SALT

2 TABLESPOONS FLOUR

Combine wafer crumbs and butter. Set aside 1/4 cup crumb mixture for topping. Pat remaining crumbs into 8-inch-square pan. Bake at 350 degrees just until lightly browned, 4 to 5 minutes. Let cool.

Beat egg substitute until thick and light in color. Gradually beat in sugar until very thick and light. Stir in lemon zest and juice, salt and flour. Pour over baked crust. Sprinkle remaining crumbs over top.

Bake at 350 degrees about 20 minutes or until center is set. Let cool to room temperature. Cut into bars or desired shapes.

18 bars. Each bar: 65 calories; 39 mg sodium; 6 mg cholesterol; 2 grams fat; 12 grams carbohydrates; 1 gram protein; 0.01 gram fiber.

ANISE MERINGUE KISSES

3 EGG WHITES
1/8 TEASPOON CREAM OF TARTAR
1/2 CUP SUGAR
1 1/2 TEASPOONS GROUND ANISE SEEDS

Beat egg whites until frothy. Add cream of tartar and beat to soft peaks. Gradually beat in sugar. Continue beating until stiff and glossy. Beat in anise. Using pastry bag, pipe onto parchment-lined baking sheets. Bake at 275 degrees 30 minutes.

About 4 dozen kisses. Each kiss: 9 calories; 4 mg sodium; 0 cholesterol; 0 fat; 2 grams carbohydrates; 0 protein; trace fiber.

> If you prefer the dry melt-in-your-mouth type, turn off the oven when the cookies are through baking and, with the door closed, let them stand 30 minutes to an hour.
>
> By the way, meringue cookies are generally baked on parchment paper, but regular bond paper makes a very acceptable and far less expensive substitute.

PINE NUT CRISPS

1 CUP GRANULATED SUGAR
1/2 CUP FLOUR
6 EGG WHITES
1 TEASPOON VANILLA EXTRACT
1/8 TEASPOON ORANGE EXTRACT
2 TABLESPOONS BUTTER, MELTED
3/4 CUP PINE NUTS
Powdered sugar

Combine granulated sugar, flour and unbeaten egg whites. Stir to blend. Add vanilla, orange extract and butter. Fold in pine nuts. Drop by tablespoons, 3 to 4 per large baking sheet, onto lightly buttered baking sheets. Spread batter in 3-inch circles, allowing ample room for spreading.

Bake at 350 degrees 8 to 10 minutes or until browned. Remove to wire rack to cool. Sprinkle with powdered sugar to taste.

2 dozen cookies. Each cookie: 79 calories; 23 mg sodium; 3 mg cholesterol; 4 grams fat; 11 grams carbohydrates; 2 grams protein; 0.05 grams fiber.

> Be sure to remove the cookies from the oven as soon as they turn golden brown and to put them on a wire rack to cool and turn crisp. If you have any difficulty lifting them off the pan, return them to the oven for a minute or two to soften.

Cookies are trouble for most fat-conscious eaters; blame it on the butter. But biscotti require less butter than most cookies.

In this recipe, the herbal flavor of the fresh rosemary is a terrific match for the sweetness of the currants.

The baking time in this recipe is designed to give the cookies a soft texture; a more traditional hard texture can be achieved by baking the biscotti a little longer.

ROSEMARY BISCOTTI

1/4 CUP BUTTER
1 1/2 CUPS SUGAR
3 EGG WHITES
1/4 CUP EGG SUBSTITUTE (EQUIVALENT TO 1 EGG)
2 TEASPOONS VANILLA EXTRACT
1/4 TEASPOON ALMOND EXTRACT
1/4 CUP MINCED FRESH ROSEMARY
1/2 CUP CURRANTS
3 CUPS FLOUR
1 TABLESPOON BAKING POWDER
1/2 TEASPOON SALT
NONSTICK COOKING SPRAY

Beat butter in mixing bowl until light and creamy. Beat in sugar until light. Beat in 2 egg whites until blended. Beat in egg substitute, vanilla extract, almond extract and 2 tablespoons minced rosemary until blended. Stir in currants.

Sift together flour, baking powder and salt in separate bowl. Stir into creamed mixture until completely mixed.

Divide dough into 2 parts. Shape each half into 12-inch log.

Roll each log in 1 tablespoon minced rosemary to coat outside. Place logs on baking sheet lightly sprayed with nonstick cooking spray. Lightly beat remaining egg white and brush tops and sides of logs. Bake at 350 degrees until lightly browned, 25 to 30 minutes.

Remove logs from oven and let cool 10 to 15 minutes. Cut each log into 1/2-inch slices. Arrange on baking sheets and bake until lightly browned, 10 to 15 minutes.

About 32 biscotti. Each biscotti: 93 calories; 99 mg sodium; 4 mg cholesterol; 2 grams fat; 18 grams carbohydrates; 2 grams protein; 0.17 gram fiber.

CHOCOLATE PUDDING WITH SLICED BANANAS

1/3 CUP COCOA
1/3 CUP SUGAR
3 TABLESPOONS CORNSTARCH
1/4 TEASPOON SALT

2 1/4 CUPS PLUS 1 CUP OPTIONAL NONFAT MILK
1 TEASPOON VANILLA EXTRACT
2 SMALL BANANAS

Combine cocoa, sugar, cornstarch and salt in large saucepan. Gradually blend in 2 1/4 cups milk. Heat to boiling, stirring constantly. Boil and stir 1 minute, until thickened and cornstarch is cooked.

Remove from heat. Stir in vanilla. Divide into serving dishes. Cover and chill. Slice 1/2 banana over each serving. Serve with extra 1 cup milk to pour over pudding.

4 servings. Each serving, without optional milk: 210 calories; 231 mg sodium; 3 mg cholesterol; 2 grams fat; 47 grams carbohydrates; 7 grams protein; 0.69 gram fiber.

> To prevent the cornstarch from clumping when the milk is added, first combine it with the cocoa, sugar and salt in a saucepan and then slowly add the milk. For the smoothest texture, stir the pudding while it is heating. After the pudding begins to simmer, cook and stir constantly—to prevent scorching—for one minute, until thickened and clear. Remove from heat, stir in vanilla, then pour into serving dishes.

BAVARIAN CREAM WITH RASPBERRY SAUCE

1 TABLESPOON UNFLAVORED GELATIN
2 TABLESPOONS COLD WATER
1 1/2 CUPS NONFAT MILK
1/4 TEASPOON SALT
1/4 CUP SUGAR

1/4 TEASPOON VANILLA EXTRACT
1/4 TEASPOON ALMOND EXTRACT
1 CUP LOW-FAT WHIPPED TOPPING
1/2 PINT RASPBERRIES

Sprinkle gelatin over cold water to soften. Heat milk to simmering. Stir in salt and 2 tablespoons sugar. Stir in softened gelatin until dissolved. Stir in vanilla and almond extracts.

Chill until slightly thickened. Fold in whipped topping. Spoon into stemmed glasses and chill until set.

Purée raspberries with remaining 2 tablespoons sugar and strain. Spoon over chilled almond cream and serve.

4 servings. Each serving: 147 calories; 213 mg sodium; 2 mg cholesterol; 3 grams fat; 26 grams carbohydrates; 6 grams protein; 1.17 grams fiber.

> Served topped with raspberry sauce, this is a light, refreshing dessert that's easy to make and looks elegant for entertaining when spooned into crystal goblets.
>
> You may prepare this dessert the day before or the day of your party.

DESSERTS

A wonderful coffee aroma and silky smooth texture are what make this custard so great.

For a strong coffee flavor, use instant espresso; for a lighter coffee flavor, use regular instant coffee. A touch of vanilla and almond extracts bring out the flavor of the coffee.

For extra flavor and a bit of crunch, try crushing a few coffee beans very finely and sprinkling them over the top of the custard just before serving.

CAFFE LATTE CUSTARD

1 CUP NONFAT EVAPORATED MILK

3 TABLESPOONS GROUND INSTANT ESPRESSO

1/2 CUP SUGAR

1 CUP NONFAT MILK

3/4 CUP EGG SUBSTITUTE (EQUIVALENT TO 3 EGGS)

2 TEASPOONS VANILLA EXTRACT

1/4 TEASPOON ALMOND EXTRACT

6 COFFEE BEANS, FINELY CRUSHED, OPTIONAL

Heat evaporated milk and instant espresso in small saucepan over medium heat, stirring until coffee is dissolved. Stir in sugar until dissolved.

Stir in nonfat milk, then egg substitute and vanilla and almond extracts.

Divide custard into 6 (6-ounce) oval baking dishes. Put filled baking dishes in large pan and add water to reach halfway up sides of mold.

Bake at 325 degrees just until custard is set, 15 to 20 minutes. Remove dishes from water bath and cool. Chill until serving time. Sprinkle crushed coffee beans over top before serving.

6 servings. Each serving: 133 calories; 114 mg sodium; 2 mg cholesterol; 0 fat; 25 grams carbohydrates; 8 grams protein; 0 fiber.

CREAMY RICE PUDDING

1/2 CUP RICE
1/2 CUP WATER
4 CUPS NONFAT MILK
1/3 CUP NONFAT DRY MILK
1 STICK CINNAMON
1/2 CUP SUGAR
1 CUP DARK OR GOLDEN RAISINS
1/4 CUP EGG SUBSTITUTE (EQUIVALENT TO 1 EGG)
1 TEASPOON VANILLA EXTRACT
GROUND CINNAMON OR NUTMEG
NONFAT MILK, WARMED, OPTIONAL

Combine rice and water in 4-quart saucepan. Bring to simmer over medium heat. Cover and cook over low heat until water is absorbed, 4 to 5 minutes.

Add milk and dry milk to rice, stirring until blended. Add cinnamon stick. Bring to boil over medium heat. Reduce heat to simmer. Cover and cook 25 to 30 minutes, until rice is tender and pudding has creamy consistency. Stir in sugar and raisins during last 10 minutes of cooking.

Combine egg substitute and little hot pudding. Add to pudding in saucepan. Heat just until custard thickens slightly, stirring constantly, 1 to 2 minutes. Remove from heat and stir in vanilla. Serve at room temperature or chilled. Sprinkle with ground cinnamon and serve with warm nonfat milk.

8 servings. Each serving, without extra nonfat milk: 221 calories; 118 mg sodium; 3 mg cholesterol; 1 gram fat; 46 grams carbohydrates; 9 grams protein; 0.28 gram fiber.

Rice pudding is one of those comfort foods I find especially satisfying when the weather cools. This recipe is easy to prepare and can be made one day ahead.

When you're ready to eat it, pop an individual serving into the microwave to warm, then sprinkle it with cinnamon or nutmeg. A drizzle of warm nonfat milk makes it even more soothing.

DESSERTS

Made in a blender, this light, tangy dessert is ready for the oven in minutes. Raw sugar is sprinkled over the top of the chilled dessert, which is then broiled to make the crackly topping.

By the way, it's worth taking the trouble to search for raw sugar crystals, which melt more quickly than regular sugar. They can be found at supermarkets and health food stores.

LEMON BRULÉE

1 CUP NONFAT MILK

1 CUP SUGAR

3/4 CUP LEMON JUICE

1 TABLESPOON GRATED LEMON ZEST

1/4 CUP FLOUR

1 (8-OUNCE) EGG SUBSTITUTE (EQUIVALENT TO 4 EGGS)

2 TABLESPOONS BUTTER, MELTED

1 TABLESPOON RAW SUGAR CRYSTALS

Combine milk, sugar, lemon juice, zest, flour, egg substitute and butter in blender. Blend 2 to 3 minutes. Pour into lightly buttered 9-inch round baking dish. Bake at 350 degrees 40 to 45 minutes or until center is set. Remove to wire rack to cool. Chill.

Just before serving, sprinkle raw sugar over top. Place under broiler until sugar is melted and top is brown.

8 servings. Each serving: 199 calories; 119 mg sodium; 34 mg cholesterol; 6 grams fat; 34 grams carbohydrates; 5 grams protein; 0.01 gram fiber.

FRESH BERRY COBBLER

FILLING

- 1/2 PINT STRAWBERRIES, HULLED AND HALVED
- 1/2 PINT BLUEBERRIES
- 1/2 PINT BLACKBERRIES
- 1/2 PINT RASPBERRIES
- 1/3 CUP GRANULATED SUGAR
- 2 TABLESPOONS QUICK-COOKING TAPIOCA
- 1 TEASPOON LIME JUICE
- 2 TEASPOONS BUTTER, MELTED
- 2 TEASPOONS BROWN SUGAR, PACKED

DROP BISCUIT SWIRL

- 1 CUP REDUCED-FAT BAKING MIX
- 1/3 CUP NONFAT MILK PLUS EXTRA FOR SERVING
- 1 TABLESPOON 4-FRUIT CONSERVE

FILLING

Toss together strawberries, blueberries, blackberries, raspberries, sugar, tapioca and lime juice in large bowl. Let stand 15 minutes. Divide into 4 1-cup ramekins. Place on baking sheet. Bake at 350 degrees 15 minutes.

DROP BISCUIT SWIRL

Combine baking mix and milk and stir until almost blended. Swirl in fruit conserve.

ASSEMBLY

Spoon Drop Biscuit Swirl batter on top of each ramekin, dividing evenly. Brush each biscuit with butter and sprinkle each with brown sugar. Continue to bake until biscuits are baked through, 10 to 15 minutes. Let cool to warm. Serve with nonfat milk, if desired.

4 servings. Each serving, without extra milk: 306 calories; 366 mg sodium; 6 mg cholesterol; 5 grams fat; 65 grams carbohydrates; 5 grams protein; 3.56 grams fiber.

Cobblers don't have to have rich, buttery toppings. By using reduced-fat buttermilk baking mix and nonfat milk, you can make a simple and delicious berry cobbler.

The tops of the biscuits are brushed with a little melted butter to improve the flavor, but if you're cutting out all possible fat, you can omit this step.

The cobbler is best served warm, with a little nonfat milk drizzled over the biscuit.

DESSERTS

The best part of this dessert is the crunch, which comes from sweetened oats.

The apples are cut into wedges rather than thin slices so they won't cook down to a mush while baking.

The apples need no additional sugar because there's enough sweetness in the topping.

Serve the dish warm with a little nonfat milk or a small scoop of nonfat frozen yogurt.

BAKED APPLE-OAT CRUNCH

3/4 CUP ROLLED OATS
1/2 CUP FLOUR
1/2 CUP LIGHT BROWN SUGAR, PACKED
1/2 TEASPOON BAKING SODA
1/2 TEASPOON CINNAMON
1/4 TEASPOON SALT
2 TABLESPOONS CANOLA OIL
2 TABLESPOONS BUTTER, CUT UP
4 PEELED AND CORED FUJI APPLES, EACH CUT INTO 12 WEDGES
1 TEASPOON LEMON JUICE
NONSTICK COOKING SPRAY

Combine oats, flour, brown sugar, baking soda, cinnamon and salt in bowl. Stir in oil. Cut in butter.

Toss together apples and lemon juice, then spoon into 1 1/2-quart baking dish sprayed with nonstick cooking spray. Sprinkle crumb mixture over top.

Bake at 350 degrees until apples are tender, 55 to 65 minutes.

8 servings. Each serving: 199 calories; 108 mg sodium; 8 mg cholesterol; 7 grams fat; 33 grams carbohydrates; 2 grams protein; 0.45 gram fiber

---

This low-fat version of my favorite Thanksgiving pie—made with nonfat milk and egg substitute—is spiced with freshly grated ginger and Chinese five-spice powder instead of the usual pumpkin pie spices.

A gingersnap crust made without butter is substituted for a pastry crust to keep the fat content low.

GINGER-PUMPKIN PIE

1 CUP CRUSHED GINGERSNAPS (ABOUT 16 GINGERSNAPS)
3/4 CUP PLUS 2 TABLESPOONS SUGAR
NONSTICK COOKING SPRAY
1 (16-OUNCE) CAN PUMPKIN
2 TEASPOONS GRATED GINGER ROOT
3/4 TEASPOON CHINESE FIVE-SPICE POWDER
1/2 TEASPOON SALT
1/2 CUP NONFAT EGG SUBSTITUTE (EQUIVALENT TO 2 EGGS)
1 1/2 CUPS NONFAT MILK

Combine gingersnaps and 2 tablespoons sugar in bowl. Pat mixture onto bottom and sides of 9-inch pie plate, lightly greased or sprayed with low-fat nonstick cooking spray. Set aside.

Combine pumpkin, remaining 3/4 cup sugar, ginger, 5-spice powder and salt in bowl until blended. Stir in egg substitute until blended. Stir in milk. Carefully pour into prepared crust.

Bake at 425 degrees for 15 minutes. Reduce heat to 350 degrees and continue to bake 40 to 50 minutes or until knife inserted in center comes out clean. Let cool.

8 servings. Each serving: 151 calories; 226 mg sodium; 5 mg cholesterol; 1 gram fat; 32 grams carbohydrates; 4 grams protein; 0.65 gram fiber.

PEACHES AND "CREAM" PIE

4 SMALL RIPE PEACHES, PEELED, HALVED AND PITTED

1 (8-INCH) LOW-FAT SWEET PIE CRUST

1/4 TEASPOON GROUND CINNAMON

1 CUP NONFAT MILK

2 TABLESPOONS NONFAT MILK POWDER

1/2 CUP NONFAT EGG SUBSTITUTE (EQUIVALENT TO 2 EGGS)

1/3 CUP SUGAR

1 TEASPOON VANILLA EXTRACT

Arrange peaches pitted side up in pre-baked pie crust. Sprinkle over cinnamon. Combine nonfat milk and nonfat milk powder, stirring until blended. Stir in egg substitute, sugar and vanilla. Pour over peaches in crust.

Bake at 350 degrees 40 to 45 minutes or until center tests done with knife. Let cool to warm. Makes 8 servings.

LOW-FAT SWEET PIE CRUST

1/2 CUP PLUS 2 TABLESPOONS OAT FLOUR BLEND

5 TABLESPOONS ALL-PURPOSE FLOUR

1/4 CUP CAKE FLOUR

1/2 TEASPOON GROUND CINNAMON

2 1/2 TABLESPOONS SUGAR

3 TABLESPOONS COLD BUTTER, DICED

1 TABLESPOON CANOLA OIL

2 TO 2 1/2 TABLESPOONS VERY COLD WATER

1 TABLESPOON EGG SUBSTITUTE

Sift flours, cinnamon and sugar into large bowl. Rub in butter with fingers or cut in with pastry cutter until size of small peas. Using fork, stir in oil. Slowly add cold water, 1 teaspoon at time, tossing with fork until flour is moistened without being wet.

Gather dough with moist hands, shape into flattened round, let rest 15 minutes. Roll 1/8-inch thick on lightly floured board to fit 8-inch pie plate. Trim and flute edges. Pierce crust all over with fork. Brush crust with egg substitute. Bake at 400 degrees about 10 minutes until crust is lightly browned. Let cool to room temperature.

8 servings Each serving: 227 calories; 102 mg sodium; 13 mg cholesterol; 7 grams fat; 38 grams carbohydrates; 6 grams protein; 0.56 gram fiber.

This pie sounds rich. It tastes rich too. But the custard filling is very low in fat and the pie crust, which is made of a blend of three flours, contains only 3 tablespoons of butter.

To ensure the best flavor, use only fully ripened peaches. To ensure the best texture in the crust, brush it with egg substitute and then pre-bake the shell to keep it from becoming soggy. Be sure to cool the crust completely before adding the filling.

DESSERTS

This pie is absolutely irresistible and extraordinarily fresh-tasting. It was picked as one of the Food Section's Top Ten recipes the year it was first published.

The recipe comes from Ardell Kochevar, the mother of former Food Section staff writer Kathie Jenkins.

Try other fresh fruits, such as raspberries or peaches, in place of the blueberries.

JUNE BLUEBERRY PIE

LOW-FAT PASTRY CRUST

- 1 CUP CAKE FLOUR
- 2 TABLESPOONS SUGAR
- 1/2 TEASPOON SALT
- 1/8 TEASPOON BAKING POWDER
- 3 TABLESPOONS BUTTER, CUT UP
- 2 TABLESPOONS EGG SUBSTITUTE (EQUIVALENT TO 1/2 EGG)
- 1 TO 1 1/2 TABLESPOONS WATER
- 1/4 TEASPOON VANILLA EXTRACT

FILLING

- 3 CUPS BLUEBERRIES
- WATER
- JUICE OF 1 LEMON
- 3/4 CUP SUGAR
- 3 TABLESPOONS CORNSTARCH
- 1 (9-INCH) LOW-FAT PASTRY CRUST, BAKED
- NON-FAT NON-DAIRY WHIPPED TOPPING
- MINT LEAVES

LOW-FAT PASTRY CRUST

Combine flour, sugar, salt and baking powder. Cut in butter until size of small peas. Combine egg substitute, water and vanilla. Stir into flour mixture with fork. Gather dough into small flattened round.

Chill for ease in handling. Roll on lightly floured board to fit 9-inch pie plate. Gently pierce bottom and sides with fork. Bake at 375 degrees 12 to 15 minutes, until lightly browned. Remove to wire rack to cool. Makes 1 (9-inch) pie shell.

FILLING

Bring to boil 1 cup berries, 2 tablespoons water, lemon juice and sugar in medium saucepan. Reduce heat to medium and stir 3 minutes. Blend together cornstarch and 3 tablespoons water until smooth. Stir into blueberry mixture.

Bring mixture to boil again, reduce heat to medium and stir until thickened and clear. Remove from heat.

Set aside few berries for garnish, then stir in remaining blueberries. Turn into cooled baked Low-Fat Pastry Crust. Chill until set. Pipe with nonfat, nondairy whipped topping. Garnish with blueberries and mint leaves.

8 servings. Each serving: 216 calories; 181 mg sodium; 12 mg cholesterol; 5 grams fat; 43 grams carbohydrates; 2 grams protein; 0.74 gram fiber.

LEMON DREAM CAKE

1 TABLESPOON BUTTER, SOFTENED
2 2/3 CUPS CAKE FLOUR
1 1/2 CUPS SUGAR
2 TEASPOONS BAKING POWDER
1 TEASPOON BAKING SODA
1 CUP NONFAT MILK
1 CUP APPLESAUCE
1/2 CUP EGG SUBSTITUTE (EQUIVALENT TO 2 EGGS)
2 TEASPOONS VANILLA
1/3 CUP FRESH LEMON JUICE
GRATED ZEST OF 2 LEMONS
2 EGG WHITES
LEMON CURD
FLUFFY LEMON FROSTING
TOASTED SLICED ALMONDS, OPTIONAL

Brush 2 (9-inch) cake pans with butter or spray with non-stick cooking spray. Sift together cake flour, sugar, baking powder and baking soda into large bowl. Set aside.

Combine nonfat milk, applesauce, egg substitute, vanilla, lemon juice and zest. Beat egg whites until stiff but not dry. Quickly fold in applesauce mixture. Fold into dry ingredients just until moistened. Pour batter into prepared cake pans. Bake at 350 degrees 25 to 30 minutes.

Let cool in pan 5 minutes. Remove to wire rack to cool. Split each cake layer in half. Assemble 4 layers, spreading 1/2 cup each Lemon Curd atop three layers and remaining 1 cup on fourth or top layer. Frost sides of cake with Fluffy Lemon Frosting. Arrange almonds around top of cake.

16 servings. Each serving: 297 calories; 176 mg sodium; 4 mg cholesterol; 2 grams fat; 68 grams carbohydrates; 4 grams protein; 0.12 gram fiber.

Recipe continues on next page

This cake looks lavish, thanks to the clouds of white frosting and the thick lemon curd filling. But look again. This versatile delight, which is fit for any special occasion, has only 2 grams of fat per serving.

Lemon Curd

7 TABLESPOONS CORNSTARCH
1 1/2 CUPS SUGAR
1/2 TEASPOON SALT
2 CUPS BOILING WATER
1/4 CUP EGG SUBSTITUTE (EQUIVALENT TO 1 EGG)
1/4 CUP LEMON JUICE
1 TABLESPOON BUTTER
1 TABLESPOON GRATED LEMON ZEST

Stir together cornstarch, sugar and salt in top saucepan of double boiler. Stir in boiling water until blended. Heat and stir directly over medium-low heat until boiling and clear.

Place saucepan over double boiler and cook 10 minutes over simmering water. Add little hot mixture to egg substitute, stirring until blended. Return to double boiler and cook 2 minutes. Stir in lemon juice, butter and lemon zest. Transfer to bowl and cool to room temperature.

Makes about 2 1/2 cups.

Fluffy Lemon Frosting

4 CUP SUGAR
2 TABLESPOONS COLD WATER
2 EGG WHITES
1/4 TEASPOON CREAM OF TARTAR
1/2 TEASPOON VANILLA
1/4 TEASPOON LEMON EXTRACT

Combine sugar, cold water, egg whites and cream of tartar in top of double boiler. Beat 30 seconds with electric mixer until blended. Beat about 7 minutes over simmering water until stiff peaks are formed. Remove from heat. Stir in vanilla and lemon extract.

Makes about 2 1/2 cups.

CHOCOLATE CARROT CAKE

2 CUPS SUGAR

1 1/3 CUPS FLOUR

2/3 CUP UNSWEETENED COCOA PLUS EXTRA FOR GARNISH

2 TEASPOONS BAKING POWDER

1 1/2 TEASPOONS BAKING SODA

1/2 TEASPOON CINNAMON

1 TEASPOON SALT

1 CUP SEEDLESS RAISINS

1/2 CUP CHOPPED WALNUTS

1 CUP EGG SUBSTITUTE (EQUIVALENT TO 4 EGGS)

2 (4-OUNCE) JARS CARROT BABY FOOD

1 (8-OUNCE) CAN CRUSHED PINEAPPLE WITH JUICE

2 CUPS SHREDDED CARROTS

NONSTICK COOKING SPRAY OR BUTTER FOR GREASING PAN

POWDERED SUGAR

Sift together sugar, flour, cocoa, baking powder, baking soda, cinnamon and salt. Sprinkle raisins and walnuts over dry ingredients.

Combine egg substitute, carrot baby food, pineapple with juice and shredded carrots in separate bowl. Stir until mixed.

Make well in center of dry ingredients. Pour carrot mixture into center and quickly stir just until all ingredients are moistened.

Pour batter into 13x9-inch baking pan that has been sprayed with nonstick cooking spray. Bake at 350 degrees until toothpick inserted in center comes out clean, 40 to 45 minutes. Let cool to room temperature. Sprinkle with powdered sugar and extra cocoa before serving.

12 servings. Each serving: 298 calories; 310 mg sodium; 0 cholesterol; 4 grams fat; 63 grams carbohydrates; 6 grams protein; 2.52 grams fiber.

It's not hard to make a low-fat carrot cake. But what about a low-fat chocolate carrot cake?

First, use unsweetened cocoa instead of Baker's chocolate and egg substitute instead of whole eggs. Baby-food carrots and crushed pineapple replace the fat used in most cakes; they also add moisture. A dusting of powdered sugar and cocoa takes the place of frosting. Do not over-mix the batter or the cake will be tough. Also, check during baking to prevent over-baking and drying.

DESSERTS

The trick here is to brush the bottom and sides of the baking pan with a little butter before sprinkling the berries in the pan to prevent the berries from sticking and to add flavor.

When making cakes without fat, it is important not to over-mix the batter, or the cakes will turn out tough and rubbery. It is also important not to over-bake the cake.

To get the best flavor, serve the cake warm.

VERY BERRY CAKE

1 TABLESPOON BUTTER, SOFTENED
1 CUP BLUEBERRIES
1 1/2 CUPS RASPBERRIES
1 CUP CAKE FLOUR
3/4 CUP SUGAR
1 1/2 TEASPOONS BAKING POWDER
1/4 CUP NONFAT EGG SUBSTITUTE
1/2 TEASPOON VANILLA EXTRACT
1/4 TEASPOON ALMOND EXTRACT
POWDERED SUGAR

Use softened butter to grease 9-inch-round baking pan. Sprinkle blueberries and 1 cup raspberries in bottom of pan.

Purée remaining 1/2 cup raspberries in food processor or blender and strain to make about 1/4 cup purée.

Stir together flour, sugar and baking powder in medium bowl. Blend together egg substitute, vanilla and almond extracts. Make well in center of flour mixture and pour in egg mixture and raspberry purée. Quickly stir together ingredients until just blended.

Spoon batter in dollops over berries in prepared pan. Spread batter evenly over berries to cover. Bake at 350 degrees until toothpick inserted in center comes out clean, 20 to 25 minutes. Let cool 5 minutes. Loosen cake around edge of pan and invert onto serving platter. Sprinkle with powdered sugar.

8 servings. Each serving: 159 calories; 105 mg sodium; 4 mg cholesterol; 2 grams fat; 35 grams carbohydrates; 2 grams protein; 0.96 gram fiber.

PINK PEPPERCORN ANGEL FOOD CAKE

1 CUP FLOUR
1 1/4 CUPS SUGAR
1/2 TEASPOON SALT
2 TEASPOONS FINELY CRUSHED PINK PEPPERCORNS
2 CUPS EGG WHITES (12 LARGE EGG WHITES)
1 1/2 TEASPOONS CREAM OF TARTAR
2 TEASPOONS VANILLA EXTRACT
RASPBERRY-MINT SAUCE

Sift together flour, 3/4 cup sugar and salt onto sheet of wax paper. Stir in crushed pink peppercorns.

Beat egg whites until foamy. Beat in cream of tartar. Gradually add remaining 1/2 cup sugar, beating only until soft, smooth peaks form. Beat in vanilla.

Sprinkle 1/2 of flour mixture over beaten whites and whisk on low speed just until flour is mixed in. Repeat with remaining flour mixture. Spoon batter into ungreased 10-inch tube pan and spread evenly. Remove air pockets by moving spatula up and down in circle around center of batter.

Bake at 325 degrees 30 minutes or until top is golden and wood pick inserted in center comes out clean. Invert pan to cool completely. Loosen sides with knife and turn cake out onto serving platter. Serve with Raspberry-Mint Sauce.

10 servings. Each serving, with raspberry-mint sauce: 209 calories; 209 mg sodium; 0 cholesterol; 0 fat; 47 grams carbohydrates; 6 grams protein; 1.15 grams fiber.

RASPBERRY-MINT SAUCE

1 (12-OUNCE) PACKAGE SLIGHTLY SWEETENED FROZEN RASPBERRIES
2 TABLESPOONS SUGAR OR TO TASTE
1 CUP FRESH RASPBERRIES
1 1/2 TABLESPOONS CHOPPED FRESH MINT LEAVES

Purée frozen raspberries in blender until smooth. Stir in sugar to taste. Fold in fresh whole berries and mint.

DESSERTS

Angel food is the most delicate of all cakes. But this angel has a bite: Hidden inside are pink peppercorns that give this no-fat cake a spicy edge. The raspberry mint sauce echoes both the color and pungency of the peppercorns.

Is it possible to cut the fat out of chocolate cake? Lots of people have tried. Few have succeeded. The problem: nothing brings out chocolate's smooth texture, that luxurious feeling it leaves on your tongue, like high-fat butter.

This chocolate cake is made with prunes, but prunes aren't what you taste. No one pretends that this is the richest or most chocolatey cake you can make, but it is among the very best-tasting low-fat chocolate cakes around.

Simply replacing one cup of butter with prune purée reduces the fat count from 17 grams to 2 grams. The percentage of calories from fat drops from 41% to 7%. And you lose more than 100 calories.

CHOCOLATE CLOUD CAKE

2 CUPS FLOUR

1 CUP UNSWEETENED COCOA POWDER

2 CUPS SUGAR

2 TEASPOONS BAKING SODA

1 TEASPOON BAKING POWDER

1/4 TEASPOON SALT

4 (2 1/2-OUNCE) JARS BABY FOOD PURÉED PRUNES

2 TEASPOONS VANILLA EXTRACT

1/2 CUP EGG SUBSTITUTE (EQUIVALENT TO 2 EGGS)

1 CUP NONFAT MILK

2 TABLESPOONS INSTANT ESPRESSO COFFEE POWDER

1 CUP BOILING WATER

NONSTICK COOKING SPRAY

Sift together flour, cocoa, sugar, baking soda, baking powder and salt into mixing bowl. Stir until blended. Add prunes, vanilla, eggs and milk and stir just until blended.

Combine espresso and boiling water and stir until dissolved. Stir into batter until blended. Pour batter into 2 (9-inch) round baking pans sprayed with cooking spray.

Bake at 350 degrees 30 to 35 minutes or until wood pick inserted in center comes out clean. Let cakes cool in pans 10 minutes. Invert onto wire rack to cool. Sprinkle each layer with powdered sugar. Cut into wedges and serve.

24 single-layer pieces. Each serving,:128 calories; 80 mg sodium; 18 mg cholesterol; 1 grams fat; 29 grams carbohydrates; 3 grams protein; 0.18 gram fiber.

AVOCADO CAKE WITH DATES

- 1 1/2 CUPS CAKE FLOUR
- 1 1/3 CUPS SUGAR
- 1/2 TEASPOON GROUND CINNAMON
- 1/2 TEASPOON GROUND NUTMEG
- 1/2 TEASPOON GROUND ALLSPICE
- 1 1/2 TEASPOONS BAKING SODA
- 1/2 TEASPOON SALT
- 1 CUP MASHED AVOCADOS (ABOUT 1 1/2 AVOCADOS)
- 1/2 CUP EGG SUBSTITUTE (EQUIVALENT TO 2 EGGS)
- 1/3 CUP NONFAT MILK
- 1 CUP CHOPPED DATES
- NONSTICK COOKING SPRAY OR BUTTER
- POWDERED SUGAR, ADDITIONAL SLIVERED DATES, OPTIONAL

Sift together cake flour, sugar, cinnamon, nutmeg, allspice, baking soda and salt in large bowl. Blend together avocados, egg substitute and nonfat milk in small bowl. Stir into dry ingredients along with dates until blended. Spread batter evenly into 9-inch square baking pan sprayed with cooking spray.

Bake at 325 degrees 25 to 30 minutes or until wood pick inserted in center comes out clean. Cool in pan. Sprinkle lightly with powdered sugar. Garnish top with few slivers of dates, if desired.

12 servings. Each serving: 217 calories; 119 mg sodium; 0 cholesterol; 4 grams fat; 46 grams carbohydrates; 3 grams protein; 0.76 gram fiber.

DESSERTS

You don't really taste avocados. Instead, the fruit provides a nicely dense, pound-cake-like texture that's normally achieved with butter. And by substituting dates for nuts, even more fat is eliminated.

Note that overbaking will cause the avocado to turn slightly bitter.

To dress the cake up, place a lacy paper doily over the cake as a stencil and sprinkle powdered sugar on top. When you remove the doily, a lacy pattern will remain.

Photographs by Los Angeles Times Staff Photographers:

Berry Blast: Iris Schneider
Oven-Fried Zucchini: Robert Durell
Caviar-Stuffed Potatoes: Anacleto Rapping
Escarole Chicken Soup: Kirk McKoy
Baja Squid Salad: Con Keyes
Shrimp and Garlic Coleslaw: Kirk McKoy
Shredded Chicken Salad: Al Seib
Winter Fruit Salad: Lawrence K. Ho
Pad Thai Noodles: Anacleto Rapping
Steamed Salmon with Tarragon Sauce: Anacleto Rapping
Chinese Rock Cod with Vegetables: Perry C. Riddle
Dilled Turkey Meat Balls: Rick Meyer
Turkey Fajitas: Gary Friedman
Savory Baked Sweet Potatoes: Gary Friedman
Eggplant Stack: Robert Gauthier
Honeydew Ice: Perry C. Riddle

Front Cover
Fresh Vegetable Toss with Wasabi Vinaigrette: Robert Gauthier
    (recipe on pg. 43)
Back Cover
Mexican Chocolate Ice: Kirk McKoy
    (recipe on pg. 100)

Index

"*n*" indicates sidebar note

adobo seasoning, 66
anchovy paste, 37
appetizers, dips, *n*, p. 37
apples, 19, 110
applesauce, in cake, 111
artichoke & shrimp salad, 44
artichoke hearts, 27

basic foods to have on hand, 11–13
beans
    black, refried, 71
    yellow, creamed, 87
beef
    choosing, 8, *n*, p. 66
    flank steak adobo, grilled, 66
    sitr-fry, 65
    to tenderize tough, *n*, p. 66
beets, roasted, in salad, 47
bell pepper, roasting method, *n*, p. 42
berry
    cake, 116
    cobbler, 109
    pie, blueberry, 119
black-eyed peas, *n*, p. 45
bread
    muffins, corn, 62
    olive-yogurt, 60
    sticks, skinny, 61
broccoli rabe (rapini), 13, *n*, p. 29
brown rice syrup, 11, *n*, p. 20
Brussels sprouts on stalk, *n*, p. 86

cakes, 113-119
cannelloni, stuffed, 55
caviar, *n*, p. 24
chayote squash, stuffed, *n*, p. 92
chicken
    enchiladas, 85
    in salad, 49, 51, *n*, p. 49
chile powder, Pasilla, *n*, p. 82
chile sauce, *n*, p. 82
chiles, 11, 27
    soup, 31
chili
    turkey, 82
chocolate
    horchata, Mexican ice, 100
    pudding with bananas, 105
coconut milk, *n*, p. 94
cookies, 101–104
corn
    cobs, 31
    muffins, 62
cornstarch, *n*, p. 105
couscous, 26
cranberries, sugared, 98
cucumbers, European, *n*, p. 51
curry, vegetable, 94
custards, 106

dates
    and filo dough cookies, 101
    in cake, 119

"egg" salad, 64
eggplant, 40, 91, 96
eggrolls, shrimp, 25
enchiladas, chicken, 85

fajitas, turkey, 80
fat, reducing amount of, 10, 11
    by roasting eggplant, *n*, p. 40
    by skimming broth, *n*, p. 33
    by using turkey, *notes*, pp. 79, 83
    by using yogurt, *n*, p. 74
    in baking, 10
    in cake frosting, *n*, p. 115
    in cakes, *notes*, pp. 115, 116, 117,
    in chicken enchiladas, *n*, p. 85
    in coleslaw, *n*, p. 43
    in cookies, 101
    in "dry-fried" eggplant, *n*, p. 91
    in garlic cream sauce, *n*, p. 86
    in pie crust, *n*, p. 110
    in pizza, *n*, p. 53
    in salad dressing, 52
    with cheese, *notes*, pp. 53, 55
    with filo dough, *n*, p. 23
    with oven-fry technique, *n*, p. 21
filo dough, 11, *n*, p. 23
fish
    choosing, 8
    codfish and potato brandade, 72
    grilled
        swordfish, *n*, p. 70
        marinated red snapper, 76
        tuna on skewers, 28
    salmon
        chowder, 35
        steamed, 68
    sauce, Thai, 59, *n*, p. 59
    stir-fried rock cod, 69
    stock, 35
    tuna
        casserole, with noodles 75
        on skewers, 28
        salad, 74
flavor enhancers, 8–10
frosting, fluffy lemon, 114
fruit purées, 10
fruit salad, 52

garlic purée, 40
grape leaves, stuffed 26
green beans, in salad, 39

haricots verts (thin green beans), 39, *n*, p. 39
herbs & spices
  adobo, 66
  basil, 27
  parsley, 27, 37
  sorrel, 12, 26
  tarragon, *68 n*, p. 68
horchata, *n*, p. 100
hummus, 63
Hungarian vegetable stew, 93

Kashi pilaf mix, 95 *n*, p. 95
kefir, 12, *n*, p. 46

labels on foods, how to read, 9
lamb, choosing, 8
lasagna, 57
lavash with tuna salad, 74
lecso, Hungarian vegetable stew, 93
lemon curd, 112
lentils, garnish for soup, *n*, p. 32

mandoline, 14
marinades, 9, 76
masa flour, *n*, p. 31
meat balls, turkey, 79, 83
meat, as condiment, 8
melon ice, honeydew, 99
mirin, 12, *notes* 28, 76
mushrooms, sautéed, *n*, p. 57
mustard greens, 45

noodles
  and tuna, casserole, 75
  pan fried (technique), 73
  Thai rice, *n*, p. 59
nutrition information on labels, 9

olive-yogurt bread, 60
orzo, 12, 38

pancakes
  apple, 19
  polenta, 18
pie
  blueberry, 112
  ginger-pumpkin, 110
  peach, 111
pie & pastry crust, 111,112
pilaf, vegetable, 95
pizza, 53
polenta, 18
pork, choosing, 8
potatoes, 17
  caviar-stuffed, 24
  frittata, 17
  and cilantro salad, 42
  and green bean salad, 39
potsticker wrappers, 13, *n*, p. 30
  in soup, 30
poultry, choosing, 8
pudding, chocolate & bananas, 105

quinoa, 12, *n*, p. 44

rapini (broccoli rabe), 13, *n*, p. 29
  soup, 29
rice
  and turkey bowl, *n*, p. 81
  brown rice drink, 20
  and fresh vegetable salad, 48
    cooking method, 48
  tomato, 93
  white fried, *n*, p. 67
rice pudding, 107
ricotta cheese, *n*, p. 57
rigatoni, with portabellos and peppers, 58

sake lees (kasu), *n*, p. 76
salad dressings
  balsamic vinegar, 52, 88
  cilantro vinaigrette, 42
  green goddess, 37

lemon vinaigrette, 44
  mixed herb, 46
  ranch-style, 37
  thousand island, 36
  wasabi vinaigrette, 43
salsa, 49
sauces
  balsamic vinegar, reduced, 88
  cream, reduced fat, 73
  dipping, 22, 28
  garlic cream, 86, 87
  pasta
    charred tomato, *n*, p. 54
    herbed tomato, 57
    pesto, 27
    porcini mushroom & tomato, *n*, p. 55
    portabello & roasted pepper, 58
  raspberry, 105
  raspberry-mint, 117
  red, for meat balls, 83
  sorrel, 27
  Swiss chard and tofu, *n*, p. 56
  wasabi dipping, 28
shellfish *see also* shrimp
  and black bean sauce, 77
  scallops, 73
shrimp
  and artichoke salad, 44
  and Chinese vegetable soup, 34
  and garlic coleslaw, 41
  appetizers, 22
  fried rice, 67
  in salad, 41, *n*, p. 38
  tostada, 71
soups
  broccoli rabe (rapini), 29
  chile, 31
  Chinese dumpling, 30
  Chinese vegetable, 34
  curried sweet potato, 32
  escarole & chicken, 33
  salmon chowder, 35
soy beverage, *n*, p. 20
soybeans in salad, *n*, p. 50
spinach pie, 23

spring roll wrappers, 13, *n*, p. 25
squash
   chayote, stuffed, 92
   roasted, 88
squid
   in chilled salad, 41
   preparation of, *n*, p. 41
steaming
   advantage of, *n*, p. 77
stir-fry
   noodles, Thai rice, 59
   rock cod with vegetables, 69
   turkey fajitas, 80
   turkey with tofu, 84
   vegetables & beef, 65
sugar, raw, *n*, p. 108
sweet potatoes
   herb roasted, 89
   selecting, *n*, p. 89
   soup, 32
Swiss chard, *n*, p. 56
syrups
   blackberry, 18
   brown rice, 11, *n*, p. 20

tahineh, 13, *n*, p. 63
tofu, 13
   fried, 59, *n*, p. 84, p. 97
   in Asian minced turkey, 84
   in "egg" salad, 64
   in pasta sauce, 56
   stuffed, *n*, p. 34
   sweet-and-sour, 97
tomato rice, 93
tomatoes, stuffed, 96
tortilla crisps, dessert, 100
turban, olive-yogurt, 60
turkey
   chili, 82
   in salad, 38
   meat balls, 79
   in red sauce, 83
   minced Asian, with tofu, 84
   soup, 29, 30
   stir-fried fajitas, 80
   tenderloin, grilled, 81
   terrine, cold, 78
vanilla wafer crumb crust, 102
vegetable
   pilaf, 95
   stew, 90, 93

vegetables, cooking method, *n*, p. 48
vinaigrette
   cilantro, 42
   lemon, 44
   roasted garlic, 47
   wasabi, 43
vinegar
   balsamic, 13, 88
   herb, 13
wok
   care of, 14
   sautéed fish in, *n*, p. 69
wraps, *n*, p. 63
wrappers
   grape leaves, 26
   potsticker, 13 *n*, p. 30
   spring roll, 13, *n*, p. 25
   tortillas, 63
   won tons, crisp, 43

yogurt, as substitute for mayonnaise, *n*, p. 74

zucchini appetizers, 21